Wiley Study Guide for 2019 Level III CFA Exam

Volume 2: Private Wealth Management & Institutional Investors

Thousands of candidates from more than 100 countries have relied on these Study Guides to pass the CFA® Exam. Covering every Learning Outcome Statement (LOS) on the exam, these review materials are an invaluable tool for anyone who wants a deep-dive review of all the concepts, formulas, and topics required to pass.

Wiley study materials are produced by expert CFA charterholders, CFA Institute members, and investment professionals from around the globe. For more information, contact us at info@efficientlearning.com.

Wiley Study Guide for 2019 Level III CFA Exam

Volume 2: Private Wealth Management & Institutional Investors

WILEY

Required CFA® Institute disclaimer:

"CFA® and Chartered Financial Analyst® are trademarks owned by CFA Institute. CFA Institute (formerly the Association for Investment Management and Research) does not endorse, promote, review or warrant the accuracy of the products or services offered by John Wiley & Sons, Inc."

Certain materials contained within this text are the copyrighted property of CFA Institute. The following is the copyright disclosure for these materials:

"Copyright 2018, CFA Institute. Reproduced and republished with permission from CFA Institute. All rights reserved."

These materials may not be copied without written permission from the author. The unauthorized duplication of these notes is a violation of global copyright laws and the CFA Institute Code of Ethics. Your assistance in pursuing potential violators of this law is greatly appreciated.

Disclaimer: John Wiley & Sons, Inc.'s study materials should be used in conjunction with the original readings as set forth by CFA Institute in the 2018 CFA Level III Curriculum. The information contained in this book covers topics contained in the readings referenced by CFA Institute and is believed to be accurate. However, their accuracy cannot be guaranteed.

ISBN 978-1-119-53086-2
V092629_100518

Contents

ABOUT THE AUTHORS

Wiley's Study Guides are written by a team of highly qualified CFA charterholders and leading CFA instructors from around the globe. Our team of CFA experts work collaboratively to produce the best study materials for CFA candidates available today.

Wiley's expert team of contributing authors and instructors is led by Content Director Basit Shajani, CFA. Basit founded online education start-up Élan Guides in 2009 to help address CFA candidates' need for better study materials. As lead writer, lecturer, and curriculum developer, Basit's unique ability to break down complex topics helped the company grow organically to be a leading global provider of CFA Exam prep materials. In January 2014, Élan Guides was acquired by John Wiley & Sons, Inc., where Basit continues his work as Director of CFA Content. Basit graduated magna cum laude from the Wharton School of Business at the University of Pennsylvania with majors in finance and legal studies. He went on to obtain his CFA charter in 2006, passing all three levels on the first attempt. Prior to Élan Guides, Basit ran his own private wealth management business. He is a past president of the Pakistani CFA Society.

There are many more expert CFA charterholders who contribute to the creation of Wiley materials. We are thankful for their invaluable expertise and diligent work. To learn more about Wiley's team of subject matter experts, please visit: www.efficientlearning.com/cfa/why-wiley/.

Study Session 5:
Private Wealth Management (I)

READING 10: MANAGING INDIVIDUAL INVESTOR PORTFOLIOS

Time to complete: 1.5 to 2 hours

Reading Summary: This is one of the most important readings in all of the Level III. Historically, the preparation of an individual investor's investment policy statement comes near the front of the morning exam with a comparatively high weight. Practice of past exams combined with well developed time management skills are essential for your success.

This lesson will provide you with the tools to:

1. Develop an *investment policy statement* for a private client by determining and taking into consideration risk tolerance, return requirements, and constraints; and
2. Determine a *strategic asset allocation* consistent with the investment policy statement for a private client.

LESSON 1: INVESTOR CHARACTERISTICS: SITUATIONAL AND PSYCHOLOGICAL PROFILING

INVESTOR PROFILING

An investment approach that considers the investor's preferences and behavioral biases may result in better adherence to the financial plan and better advisor-client relationships. This often starts with situational profiling.

> Note that this reading has been part of the CFA Program much longer than the three detailed readings on behavioral finance. As such, the following paragraphs on situational profiling and psychological profiling my seem out of place, but consider them as yet another way that we can get to know our clients.

LOS 10a: Discuss how source of wealth, measure of wealth, and stage of life affect an individual investors' risk tolerance. Vol 2, pp 162–165

Situational Profiling

Many different methods of *situational profiling* exist to help advisors categorize clients, address issues most important to their investment success, and develop an optimal accumulation strategy. Profiling runs the risk, however, of over-simplifying investors into distinct categories where, in fact, a particular investor may be suited to multiple categories.

Source of Wealth

An investor that built a fortune (created wealth) tends to have higher risk tolerance than investors who inherit the money or otherwise have accumulated it through passive means (e.g., 401(k) contributions, inheritance, etc.). Along with the higher risk tolerance, however, entrepreneurs may also have control or other behavioral biases that make them more difficult or resistant to work with in the investment process. Passive recipients of wealth may also have various biases (e.g., endowment bias) that must be addressed in the investment process, as well.

Measure of Wealth

Ego, lifestyle, and a variety of other factors make it difficult to measure "wealth" for purposes of categorizing investors. An elected politician with what many would consider substantial assets may consider him- or herself, through association with the world's ultra-rich and influential figures, on the doorsteps of poverty. An investor with a lavish lifestyle may not be able to remain self-sufficient through retirement even with a substantial portfolio. There have been numerous examples of sports figures who declare bankruptcy even after financially successful careers when their earnings no longer support their lifestyle.

Stage of Life

Theoretically, a person's *willingness* to accept risk should be driven by cash flow (revenue less expenses) while their *ability* to accept risk begins at a high level in youth and gradually declines through retirement toward death. Childhood and life experiences, initial level of wealth, personal ability, and ambitions all combine to individualize each investor's risk tolerance.

The following four phases constitute the *investor life cycle* and can influence each investor's policy toward risk:

You are responsible for knowing these stages as well as others identified by learning outcomes elsewhere in the curriculum.

1. *Foundation phase*—Investors in this phase are usually young and thus have long time horizons. They establish their base for income generation in this phase, often by developing a marketable skill, obtaining a college education, or starting a business. Investors with inherited wealth should certainly embrace higher risk levels than those for whom any loss could be catastrophic. Family dynamics may result in a desire for greater wealth accumulation, although situational dynamics may prevent the ability or willingness to assume risk.

2. *Accumulation phase*—The groundwork from the foundation phase begins to pay off in this stage as income increases and investment assets accumulate. In the early segment of this phase, expenses may also increase and the investor has a family, purchases a home, and pays or helps pay for their children's education. In the later segment of this phase, children may become independent and expenses may decrease. The investor may consider downsizing their living accommodations at this point, although some clients may prefer to increase spending on luxury items or conspicuous consumption. Savings may increase as income outpaces expenses. Risk tolerance may increase during this phase.

3. *Maintenance phase*—This phase focuses on maintaining the lifestyle achieved during the accumulation phase, often with the individual selling a business or living off of accumulated funds. Growth of wealth declines in importance; risk tolerance decreases. Other than portfolio stability, the chief challenge may be to preserve purchasing power of the accumulated assets from the previous phase.

4. *Distribution phase*—Individuals in this phase often decide to transfer unneeded accumulated wealth to other people or entities. Individuals, especially those with substantial wealth, will often make careful plans to take advantage of market conditions, tax laws, and transfer mechanisms such as trusts and insurance programs. Planning advanced healthcare directives, gifting, and changes in legal ownership of assets may also be prudent.

Progression from the foundation to distribution phase may not always take a straight path. For example, those in the accumulation phase may return to the foundation phase for a new, more satisfying or higher paying career. Those in the maintenance phase may be forced out of retirement as the result of market conditions or unanticipated inflation. Investors in the accumulation phase who have chosen a lavish lifestyle may never leave that phase. Investors with substantial assets may not have a lower risk tolerance as they progress toward the distribution phase.

LOS 10b: Explain the role of situational and psychological profiling in understanding an individual investor's attitude toward risk. Vol 2, pp 165–171

LOS 10c: Explain the influence of investor psychology on risk tolerance and investment choices. Vol 2, pp 165–171

Psychological Profiling

Investment advisors can determine an investor's personality type and, thus, their risk tolerance and decision-making style. This can be achieved by either an ad hoc analysis by the advisor or via a questionnaire, such as that developed based on work by Bailard, Biehl, and Kaiser (BBK). There are four personality types under this model that you are responsible for recognizing on the exam, as shown in Exhibit 1-1.

Exhibit 1-1: Four Investor Personality Types

	Decisions Based on Thinking	Decisions Based on Feeling
More risk averse	**METHODICAL** • Relies on hard facts • Follows analysts or conducts own research on trading strategies • Not emotionally attached to investments because of reliance on analysis and databases • Disciplined and conservative	**CAUTIOUS** • Strong need for security from current or past experiences • Preference for low-volatility investments (principal protection) • Dislikes losing small amounts • Overanalyzes and misses opportunities • Portfolio low turnover
Less risk averse	**INDIVIDUALIST** • Self-assured and hardworking • Considers information from various sources • Takes action by him- or herself	**SPONTANEOUS** • Always adjusting portfolio holdings following the market or second-guessing self • Doubtful of investment advice • Highest portfolio turnover • Most investors have below-average returns • Quick to make decisions • More concerned about missing a trend than with portfolio risk

THE INVESTMENT POLICY STATEMENT

LOS 10d: Explain potential benefits, for both clients and investment advisers, of having a formal investment policy statement. Vol 2, pp 171–172

An *investment policy statement* (IPS) establishes the policies by which the advisor will consider the investor's life circumstances, return objectives, risk objective, and as many as five constraints. The IPS also sets portfolio construction guidelines and establishes monitoring and review parameters.

Drafting the IPS can help educate the client to recognize appropriate investment opportunities. The finished document can clarify and support the advisor's recommendations should there be questions, and provides a roadmap that the client can use with other advisors should the need arise.

LESSON 2: INDIVIDUAL IPS: RETURN OBJECTIVE CALCULATION

LOS 10e: Explain the process involved in creating an investment policy statement. Vol 2, pp 172–175

LOS 10f: Distinguish between required return and desired return and explain how these affect the individual investor's investment policy. Vol 2, pp 172–175

LOS 10g: Explain how to set risk and return objectives for individual investor portfolios and discuss the impact that ability and willingness to take risk have on risk tolerance. Vol 2, pp 172–175

Return Objective and Risk Considerations

The process of formulating return requirements for meeting client objectives also provides an educational process about the client's willingness and ability to tolerate risk.

Return Objective

A return objective may include a return required to achieve critical or primary long-term financial objectives as well as an *aspirational return* component designed to achieve a lifestyle to which the investor aspires. The advisor should discuss required and aspirational returns in the context of the investor's tolerance for risk; the aspirational return will likely be shelved if the investor cannot tolerate even the risk required for a maintenance return.

Although income and growth goals have traditionally been identified as income and growth requirements, these terms can be too easily confused with the associated assets. For example, income producing investments (e.g., low-risk Treasury securities, corporate bonds, etc.) typically have lower risk than growth-oriented investments (e.g., stocks). When inflation expectations are factored into the return requirement, however, even a "low-risk" income producing portfolio will require growth of the income component.

A total return approach, however, establishes an appropriate after-tax return on a diversified portfolio of assets that will meet the investor's goals:

- An investor with a risk tolerance too low to generate the required return must reconsider their objectives or, if able, accept a higher risk level. As an example, an investor who will have insufficient assets at the current return/risk setting to fund a child's top-tier college education may have to provide only part of the money, send the child to a lower-tier school, or increase the risk setting for their asset allocation. This latter choice, however, may result in objectionable decisions by the investor when the risk has become overwhelming to bear.
- An investor with a projected surplus over the objective accumulation can either lower the risk setting on the asset allocation to protect their objective return or increase it (to achieve even greater aspirational returns).

LESSON 3: INDIVIDUAL IPS: RISK OBJECTIVE

Risk Tolerance

An investor's risk tolerance depends not only on their *ability* to assume risk, but their *willingness* to do so. This risk tolerance translates into a risk objective for the portfolio. Investment advisors face the challenge of defining the investor's risk tolerance into a quantifiable measure.

Ability to accept risk becomes above average as:

- Time horizon and asset values increase. An investor with financial goals comprising a small portion of the assets will be better *able* to accept risk (volatility) and meet goals with a diminished portfolio value. In addition to a long time horizon, past morning exams have tended to include other information that would cause an investor's ability to take risk to be above average: being in good health, living in a country with free health care, no dependents (or financially independent dependents), and having no debt. All of these allow the investor to have more flexibility.
- Goal importance decreases. Critical goals, such as financial security or maintaining current lifestyle, generally require greater margin for error and, thus, less portfolio risk. Important, but not critical, goals may be funded with higher risk assets and, if appropriate, aspiration goals may be funded with higher risk assets.

Advisors will experience more difficulty quantifying *willingness* to accept risk. No absolute measure of "willingness" exists and, if it could be determined, it would likely change over time. The subjective willingness to accept risk will most likely appear after the portfolio has experienced both gains and losses although it will continue to remain unquantified. Watch for implied willingness to take risk from current portfolio holdings. An investor fully invested in cash or low duration assets would have a below-average willingness to take risk, while an investor 100% invested in equities would have an above-average willingness to take risk.

LESSON 4: INDIVIDUAL IPS: THE FIVE CONSTRAINTS

LOS 10h: Discuss the major constraint categories included in an individual investor's investment policy statement. Vol 2, pp 176–185

Constraints

The IPS will also identify *constraints* (i.e., economic and operational restrictions) on the portfolio, generally includable in the areas of liquidity, time horizon, tax considerations, legal and regulatory considerations, and unique circumstances.

Liquidity

In the exam, think that liquidity means the allocation to cash.

Common liquidity requirements include:

- *Ongoing expenses*—Highly predictable and often recurring costs such as daily living expenses that the investor must meet from highly liquid assets in the portfolio.
- *Emergency reserves*—A cushion against unexpected events such as loss of employment or uninsured losses, often ranging from three months to a year of ongoing expenses.
- *Negative liquidity events*—Major changes in ongoing expenses, or scheduled events such as home repairs, a child's education expense, or significant charitable donations. Liquidity needs increase as the time horizon to such events decreases.

Positive liquidity events (e.g., gifts from others and inheritance money) should also be noted in the IPS.

Real estate, limited partnerships, non-public common shares, and other illiquid assets should be specifically noted in the IPS. The IPS should also address the investment role of the family residence, specifically with regard to how the family recognizes it (i.e., intergenerational family estate vs. purely investment-related). Real estate values may be difficult to predict far into the future so it should be used with caution as a funding source for retirement, especially at a distant horizon.

If the home is to be retained from generation to generation, it is excluded from investment assets allocated as part of the investment portfolio. Other investors may view it as a source of funding for future long-term healthcare costs. Although considered a long-term funding source, the home may be a source of short- and intermediate-term expenses that must be considered, such as repairs and maintenance, insurance, etc. Any use of products that release the equity in the home (e.g., second mortgages, reverse mortgages, etc.) should be considered for their impact on the overall efficiency and effectiveness of meeting the investor's needs.

Time Horizon

Time horizon refers to the period that assets must be invested until used for some investor purpose. While short term is generally thought of as less than 3 years and long term is generally greater than 15 years, with intermediate between 3 and

15 years, the categories are somewhat flexible and must be clarified with the investor. Investment time frames often correspond to stages of the investor life cycle, with some investors having many stages and other investors having but one. In a multigenerational context, time horizon will be specific to each person considered part of the plan. When preparing your answers during the morning session of the exam, try not to be too detailed about the length of the time horizon. An investor 45 years old who plans to retire at age 65 would have a long-term, multi-stage time horizon. The first stage is between age 45 and retirement, while the second stage is between retirement and the investor's death.

Tax Considerations

Although taxes are global, a discussion of taxes necessarily must be broad rather than discuss nuances within each country. Generally, taxes fall into the following categories:

- *Income tax*—Usually a tax levied against wages, rents, dividends, and interest earned, and often with different rates applicable at different levels of income.
- *Capital gains tax*—Taxes applicable to asset price appreciation, including financial assets, with a minimum holding period often leading to a reduced tax rate.
- *Wealth transfer tax*—Taxes paid against inheritances, usually at death, or against gifts if made during the benefactor's life.
- *Property tax*—Taxes usually assessed annually against the reported value of property (or possibly against financial assets).

The magnitude of taxes against these items should provide investors with incentive to consider the *after-tax returns* from investments. Taxes affect the portfolio by:

- A single, one-time reduction in asset value (e.g., a wealth transfer tax against intergenerational transfers or a capital gains tax upon sale of an asset); and
- An ongoing reduction to portfolio value that affects accumulation (e.g., income tax and property tax).

Tax avoidance can generally be described as an attempt to pay less in tax through legal means, contrasted with *tax evasion*, which implies illegal avoidance. Everything else equal, a one-time tax at the end of the accumulation period is better for investors because it does not interfere with accumulation of untaxed amounts as does an annual or periodic tax. Therefore, a *tax deferral* strategy that postpones recognition of gain can help investors accumulate greater amounts of capital by reducing the periodic tax burden. Tax deferral often occurs when authorities wish to provide incentives for accumulation, such as with 401(k) or IRA accounts, or may simply be implemented through requirement of a minimum holding period (i.e., six months or one year). Municipal bonds and other tax exempt securities offer exemption from some or all taxes on earnings during the holding period while providing a lower cost of capital to the municipality. *Loss harvesting*, in which investors take losses in investments with a capital loss, may be useful in offsetting gains. Special loss harvesting rules may prevent repurchasing the liquidated security within some period after the sale.

Investment advisors should have a working knowledge of estate planning so they can recognize when clients should engage an estate planning specialist. Strategies for addressing wealth transfer are often country specific, but generally fall into the categories of legal structure (i.e., trusts, partnerships, etc.) and timing (inter vivos vs. testamentary). *Inter vivos* (before death) transfers decrease the amount received by heirs, and may significantly reduce the tax liability versus a *testamentary* (after death) transfer. Gifts directly to grandchildren may avoid taxation on the parents' deaths, often accomplished through an intergenerational trust that manages the assets until the grandchild reaches the age to receive the trust benefit.

Legal and Regulatory Considerations

The legal and regulatory considerations in the IPS should include a discussion of laws and regulations governing the portfolio, as well as how likely regulatory changes might impact the portfolio. Regulatory environments vary among countries, and an advisor should consult with a local expert before formulating international aspects of the IPS.

Unique Circumstances

Unique circumstances are those conditions specific to a particular client that may not apply to all of an advisor's clients. Such circumstances might include:

- Preferences for "green" investing;
- Prohibitions against investment in firms related to alcohol, tobacco, firearms, etc.;
- Assets legally restricted from sale;
- Directed brokerage;
- Privacy concerns; or
- Guidelines for special or social purpose investing.

In addition, an investor may have preferences to invest or not to invest in certain asset classes or assets within an asset class (e.g., due to previous poor experiences, etc.).

LESSON 5: A COMPLETE INDIVIDUAL IPS

LOS 10i: Prepare and justify an investment policy statement for an individual investor. Vol 2, pp 185–187

CASE STUDY

The following case study is more detailed than what you will need to know for the exam. However, we include it to illustrate the various components of the IPS.

Ellen Day manages private client accounts for a large investment firm on a politically stable island that ties its currency to the U.S. dollar. GDP has grown at a real rate of 4 percent for many years, and inflation has averaged 3 percent over the same period. The island paradise also has relatively low tax rates of 20 percent on personal income of permanent residents regardless of where earned, a 15 percent net capital gains tax on assets owned by residents with no distinction between short-and long-term gains, and a 20 percent tax on gifts and bequests (i.e., inheritance) payable *by the beneficiary,* but with the basis stepped up to avoid capital gains prior to transfer.

By contrast, South Africa's income tax burden on the wealthy is among the highest in the world, and the government has considered a "wealth" tax on incomes over ZAR 1 million (approximately USD 93,275). The South African tax code also provides that:

Capital gains tax (CGT) is also not payable by the recipient of an inheritance. Estate duty of 20 percent of the net estate amount in excess of ZAR 3,500,000 (approximately USD 326,000) is payable by the estate. Capital gains taxes of 15 percent are due on estate property liquidated prior to gifting or bequest. If it is a foreign estate, it will be subject to the taxes of its country of origin.

Day's firm has recently acquired the accounts of an investments "boutique" that specialized in attracting money from people interested in retiring to the island. Management of the acquired firm's accounts had been loose, and many of the clients had no investment policy statement (IPS). Day has been asked to manage the Steyn family account, one of the clients with no formal IPS.

In her initial conversations with Jorus and Barbara Steyn, Day learned that they will leave the assets to the children in a manner to be determined. However, they do not wish to interfere in how the children manage the assets after they have been inherited. Day, therefore, has made a decision not to profile the children at this time.

The Steyn Family
Jorus and Barbara Steyn recently celebrated their 30th anniversary at their home on the island along with their boys Ryker and Stephen, ages 29 and 27, respectively. Their daughter Amber, age 25, is an associate in a large consulting firm in London and was unable to attend the family reunion. The Steyn family will meet with Day to discuss their investments and possibly plan in more detail for their retirement in five years when Jorus turns 60 and Barbara will be 55.

Jorus Steyn founded the first in a chain of successful Steyn Auto dealerships while still in his late 20s, beginning in Johannesburg, South Africa, and stretching eastward through larger towns all the way to the Mozambique border. The five immediate family members are the sole shareholders of Steyn Auto. A large consortium has made an offer to acquire the company's equity for the equivalent of approximately USD 50 million. Jorus has lately become excited about selling his business and relaxing with Barbara on the island. They expect to travel extensively throughout the rest of the world.

Barbara Steyn comes from a wealthy family in Nelspruit, where she met Jorus as he opened his seventh dealership many years ago. Her family was killed in an automobile accident last year, and the current valuation for her share of the estate after wealth taxes is approximately USD 1.5 million. These investments currently provide annual income equivalent to USD 50,000. Barbara has convinced Jorus to immediately donate USD 10 million to the island private hospital, which has been judiciously managed, and leave the remainder of the estate to the children.

Their island home is worth USD 350,000 at current market value, a gain of USD 50,000 over what they paid a few years ago. Their mansion in South Africa is worth USD 1,500,000 at current market value, a gain of USD 1,000,000 over what they paid 10 years ago. Annual living expenses are currently USD 150,000.

The two boys are unmarried, although Ryker, currently Steyn Auto's chief financial officer, admitted while at the anniversary party he was considering marrying his long-time girlfriend Anya. Brother Stephen enjoys the single life. He attempted to enter professional golf after a successful college career at Florida State University but failed to get his U.S. PGA tour card after several attempts. He has, to his credit, worked hard on the Web.com Tour with mixed success. He has decided to seek membership in the PGA of South Africa or possibly go into golf instruction, perhaps even opening a golf school with the help of family money.

Jorus had originally intended for Ryker to become CEO of the auto dealerships and daughter Amber would become CFO. Ryker admitted last year, however, that he was interested in other entrepreneurial pursuits and wouldn't mind being cashed out of the family business.

Exhibit 5-1: Steyn Family Data (USD Equivalent)

Annual income:		
Jorus salary[1]	350,000	
Ryker salary	175,000	
Amber salary	125,000	(paid by her employer)
Barbara	50,000	(income from inheritance assets)
Joint Assets—Jorus & Barbara		
SA home, fully paid	1,500,000	
Island home, fully paid	350,000	
Yacht	350,000	
Financial assets:		
Equity securities	1,000,000	
Fixed income	350,000	
Cash	650,000	
Gold bullion	1,500,000	
Personal Assets—Jorus		
Steyn Auto equity[2]	40,000,000	
Steyn Auto equity[2]	40,000,000	
Personal Assets—Barbara		
Inheritance	1,500,000	
Steyn Auto equity[2]	5,500,000	
Personal Assets—Ryker		
Home, fully paid	350,000	
Steyn Auto equity[2]	2,500,000	
Personal Assets—Stephen		
Condominium, fully paid	250,000	
Steyn Auto equity[2]	1,000,000	
Personal Assets—Amber		
House, fully paid	350,000	(Owned jointly with spouse)
Steyn Auto equity[2]	1,000,000	

[1]Jorus will begin receiving fixed annual payments equivalent to USD 100,000 in current value from the Steyn Auto pension plan beginning in 5 years. This pension payment will be indexed annually to compensate for inflation and is currently taxable to the recipient at the standard income tax rate of 30.9 percent for their bracket.

[2]Steyn Auto equity does not pay a dividend and is stated pretax with zero cost basis for capital gains tax purposes.

Exhibit 5-2: Investment Advisor Findings and Personal Observations

Jorus

Jorus is a gregarious salesperson with a live-and-let-live attitude. He is only somewhat concerned with preserving wealth now that he has attained financial success. He attributes much of his career success to his ability to assume risk and prevail over outside forces. He comes from a long line of risk takers willing to bear adversity. Jorus' gold bullion fortune, for example, was passed on from his father (without claiming it as part of any estate) and according to family history should be used only in the event of dire emergency. Jorus was not averse to succession planning, but with the news that Ryker has no interest in continuing to run Steyn Auto has embraced the proposed acquisition.

Jorus would like to maintain his current standard of living and has no doubt his assets will provide income necessary to accomplish that. When they sell their home in South Africa and move to the island, Jorus and Barbara would like to upgrade to an estate-style luxury villa that will cost approximately USD 7.5 million.

Jorus is a "Spontaneous" personality type.

Barbara

While more detail oriented than Jorus, she has shared his passion for Steyn Auto and the excitement of assuming sometimes breathtaking financial risk. The political situation in South Africa has moved against the wealthy, in her opinion, and she desperately hopes to move to her dream villa on the politically stable island sooner rather than later. She has been actively managing the investment portfolio, but prefers more income-producing investments to offset the Steyn Auto equity holding. Barbara is pleased that the acquisition came in at such a generous pre-tax amount.

Barbara will likely visit her children extensively, wherever in the world the two boys should decide to locate. She suspects Ryker will move to the United States and Stephen will continue to live in South Africa. Amber and her husband will probably stay in London for now, although a future move is always possible. Barbara would like to maintain a bit of cash on hand to travel the world with Jorus and fund education expenses for any grandchildren that may arrive. She has no current estimate of when grandchildren might appear.

Barbara is an "Individualist" personality type.

Exhibit 5-3: Cash Flow Statement for Jorus and Barbara Steyn (USD Equivalent)

	Current	1	2	3	4	5
Inflows						
Salary—Jorus[1]	350,000	—	—	—	—	—
Pension—Jorus[1]	—	—	—	—	—	115,927
Inheritance— Barbara[2]	50,000	50,000	50,000	50,000	50,000	50,000
Sale of SA residence[3]	—	1,500,000	—	—	—	—
Sale of island residence[3]	—	350,000	—	—	—	—
Sale of company[3]		50,000,000				
Total inflows	400,000	51,900,000	50,000	50,000	50,000	165,927
Outflows						
Income tax	123,600	10,000	10,000	10,000	10,000	45,821
Gains tax[3]	—	7,657,500	—	—	—	—
Purchase villa	—	7,500,000	—	—	—	—
Living and miscellaneous[4]	150,000	154,500	159,135	163,909	168,826	173,891
Total outflows	273,600	15,322,000	169,135	173,909	178,826	219,713
Net additions/withdrawals	126,400	36,578,000	(119,135)	(123,909)	(128,826)	(53,786)

[1]Taxed at the 30.9 percent income tax rate in South Africa. Jorus' pension will derive from a South African company, and will therefore be subject to tax at that country's rate although received on the island.

[2]Taxed at 30.9 percent income tax in South Africa or 20 percent income tax rate on the island, depending where assets are held. This assumes they remain in South Africa.

[3]Taxed at the 15 percent capital gains tax rate: $[(1,000,000 + 50,000 + 50,000,000) \times .15]$.

[4]Assumed to increase at the 3 percent inflation rate.

Exhibit 5-4: Required Return Calculation—Jorus and Barbara Steyn I (USD Equivalent)

	Amount	% of Net Worth
Available Assets		
Year 1 cash flow	36,578,000	74.5
Barbara inheritance	1,500,000	3.1
Equity securities	1,000,000	2.0
Fixed income	350,000	0.7
Cash	650,000	1.3
Gold bullion	1,500,000	3.1
Investable assets	41,578,000	84.7
Island home (note that the home is excluded from the investable assets)	7,500,000	15.3
Total net worth	49,078,000	100.0
Return objective		
Distributions from the investable assets portfolio in year 2	119,135	
Real return		0.29% (119,135 / 41,578,000)
Investable assets	41,578,000	
Inflation		3.00%
Return objective		3.29%

Exhibit 5-5: Proposed Asset Allocation Alternatives—Jorus and Barbara

Asset Class	Projected Return	Standard Deviation	Allocation (%)			
			A	B	C	D
Cash equivalents	3.5	2.0	20	10	10	5
Corporate bonds	5.5	10.5	20	20	15	10
Municipal bonds	7.0	11.0	20	20	10	5
U.S. stocks: Large-cap	12.5	15.0	15	15	15	15
U.S. stocks: Small-cap	14.0	16.5	10	15	20	20
International stocks (EAFE)	15.5	21.0	10	10	15	20
REITs	10.5	15.0	5	5	10	10
Venture capital	25.0	45.0	0	5	5	15
Total	100	100	100	100		
Portfolio						
Total return	8.6	10.2	11.2	13.7		
After-tax total return	6.4	7.6	8.4	10.2		
Standard deviation	7.5	10.5	12.1	17.1		
Sharpe ratio	0.678	0.632	0.637	0.595		

Exhibit 5-6: Investment Policy Statement Prepared for Jorus and Barbara Steyn

BACKGROUND

Jorus and Barbara Steyn own and operate Steyn Auto, a multi-jurisdictional auto sales firm in South Africa. The Steyns have received a USD equivalent 50 million cash offer from a larger company for their and their children's equity in the company. These proceeds will be subject to capital gains tax on the full amount. The children are financially secure and require no additional help from Jorus and Barbara.

They wish to gift unneeded amounts of their estate up to USD 10 million to the island hospital. The remainder of the estate will be left to their children.

RETURN OBJECTIVES

The investment portfolio, less Jorus' modest retirement income and Barbara's inheritance investment asset income, must provide for their modest living expenses. In addition, portfolio growth should cover expected inflation (assumed to be 3% annually). Thus, the return objective is:

Distributions in year 2	119,135	
Investable assets	41,578,000	0.29%
Inflation		3.00%
Return objective		3.29%

RISK TOLERANCE

Following the sale of Steyn Auto, the Steyns' investment portfolio can accommodate considerable volatility without endangering its ability to meet their financial requirements. Given the considerable assets after the Steyn Auto sale, their ability to take risk appears to be "above average."

The Steyns are relatively aggressive by nature, with Jorus more so than Barbara. Personality typing shows Jorus to be "Spontaneous" and Barbara to be "Individualist." Jorus is practical, however, and has continued to hold the family's gold bullion rather than reinvest it in Steyn Auto. Overall, the Steyns are willing to accept between 10 and 15 percent fluctuation in portfolio value over a 12-month period. Their willingness to accept risk could best be described as "above average."

Their above-average ability to take risk with their above-average willingness to accept risk results in a portfolio described as having "above-average risk."

Constraints

Some constraints placed upon the assets include:

• Unnecessary assets donated to island hospital	USD 10,000,000
• Gold bullion remains intact	1,500,000
• Annual expenses subject to 3% inflation	119,135
• New house to be purchased on island	7,500,000
• Steyn Auto to be liquidated	
• House in South Africa to be sold	
• House on island to be sold	

After selling existing homes and purchasing the new home, they will have an illiquid asset equal to approximately 15.3 percent of net worth.

The bullion may also be difficult to transport from South Africa to the island.

Time Horizon

The events listed previously are expected to occur in the short-term. Jorus' pension income begins longer term (in five years), but this income will not be required to meet expenses. The time horizon is considered long-term in nature, with two stages: between now and when the portfolio stabilizes and until the death.

Taxes

The Steyns are subject to their country's tax code, although much of the asset repositioning will occur at the capital gains tax rate. This rate is the same in South Africa and the island nation, so no disadvantage accrues to repositioning the assets now. They would like to position inheritable assets to make optimal use of any tax advantages available.

Legal and Regulatory

There is nothing stated in the case about legal and regulatory constraints. However, the investment advisor would be subject to CFA Institute Code and Standards of Professional Conduct relating to managing client assets. We could also say that the advisor would most likely be subject to the prudent investor rule, a relatively high standard compared with other investor types.

Unique Circumstances

- The Steyn's plan revolves around successful disposition of Steyn Auto. This should be continually monitored to ensure progression toward a conclusion.
- The Steyns have decided not to consider their new villa, representing a large percentage of their overall net worth, as part of investable assets.
- It may be possible to gift assets to the hospital via various estate planning methods that would not involve paying a tax on the USD 10 million. This will potentially increase the Steyn's post-gifting investable assets.
- Estate planning should be considered to pass the remaining assets to the children in a tax favorable way.
- Attitudes and circumstances may change abruptly as the Steyns make these lifestyle changes. The investment strategy should remain flexible to consider these potential attitude shifts.

An analyst working with Day has provided four asset allocation scenarios presented in Exhibit 5-5. The analyst notes that there is considerable uncertainty about REIT returns, with outsize returns likely as the housing market recovers. This could be especially true if some of the large distressed property REITs perform well.

Because Barbara and Jorus have a relatively low return requirement, all of the asset allocation options will meet the required return. Portfolio D, however, is inconsistent with the 15 percent risk tolerance specified by the Steyn's IPS and must be excluded. The Steyns suggested no investment constraints that would prevent any of the allocation options. Portfolio C remains as the option with the highest return given their risk preference, and Portfolios A through C are all fairly close in terms of risk-adjusted return, declining somewhat as return increases. Portfolio C, however, has greater exposure to REITs and could have greater return than expected with little downside given current economic conditions.

LESSON 6: ASSET ALLOCATION CONCEPTS: THE PROCESS OF ELIMINATION

This assignment and the techniques explained below also apply to institutional investors, not just an individual investor as specified by the LOS. In fact, it was tested in 2009 in the context of an institutional investor. In other words, the client type does not matter; how you apply it does.

LOS 10i: Prepare and justify an investment policy statement for an individual investor. Vol 2, pp 185–187

LOS 10j: Determine the strategic asset allocation that is most appropriate for an individual investor's specific investment objectives and constraints. Vol 2, pp 188–196

ASSET ALLOCATION

Determining the most appropriate strategic asset allocation requires that the client's return, risk objectives, and investment constraints have already been formed. In addition, capital market expectations (CME) also have already been computed. Here, the examiners would provide you with CMEs for common asset classes aggregated into as many as five proposed portfolios, such as those shown in Exhibit 6-1.

Exhibit 6-1: Proposed Asset Allocation Alternatives

	Proposed Allocations				
	A (%)	B (%)	C (%)	D (%)	E (%)
Asset Class					
Cash equivalents	5	10	15	10	5
Corporate bonds	15	20	10	20	20
Government bonds	50	30	20	30	25
Large-cap stocks	25	25	45	15	10
Small-cap stocks	5	5	5	10	40
Hedge funds	0	10	5	15	0
Total	100	100	100	100	100
Summary data					
Expected total return	7.37	8.36	8.25	9.43	10.23
Expected standard deviation	9.52	10.45	10.91	11.45	12.75
Sharpe ratio (risk-free rate is 2%)	0.564	0.609	0.606	0.649	0.645

You can assume that these numbers are nominal and pre-tax. You might need to convert the returns to real (by subtracting expected inflation) and after-tax by multiplying the real result by the client's tax rate.

On the exam, you will most likely be given a series of investment policy statement information for a client, such as:

- The client has an investable asset base of $100,000, has no sources of income other than the portfolio, and has ongoing expenses of $8,000 per year. The minimum return objective is 8% per year.
- The client's minimum return threshold is –13%, expressed as two standard deviations below the expected return.
- Due to past poor investment experience, the client wishes to establish a maximum exposure to alternative investments of 10%.

To determine which portfolio allocation is the most appropriate for the client, follow a four-step process of elimination:

1. **Return objective.** Eliminate portfolios with return below the client's minimum return.
2. **Quantifiable risk.** Eliminate portfolios riskier than specified by the client.
3. **Constraints.** The most likely constraints would be related to liquidity (the need for cash) as well as any stated or implied unique constraints.
4. **Only if there is a tie, chose the portfolio with the highest risk-adjusted performance measure.** A common risk-adjusted metric is the Sharpe ratio. But only conduct this step if there is a tie. Do not go for this step if you can eliminate portfolio choices using steps 1 through 3.

> If you can clearly identify a portfolio that does not fit, then it can be eliminated.

Let's consider the proposed allocation in the context of what we know about our client.

First, we can **eliminate Portfolio A** because its return is below 8%.
Second, based on the client's implied liquidity requirement, we can **eliminate Portfolio E** because the cash allocation is too low. Because the client has no other source of income, the client needs to maintain at least 8% of the portfolio in cash to meet ongoing needs.
Third, we can **eliminate Portfolio D** because its exposure to hedge funds (alternative investment) is above the maximum of 10%.
So, we are now left with **Portfolios B and C**. We can now calculate the downside risk associated with these two portfolios. The client has stated a willingness to accept at most a downside of -13% within two standard deviations of the expected mean:

> On the exam, if the Sharpe ratio is not calculated for you, then you would only need to calculate it for any remaining portfolios, **but only in the case of a tie**. Recall that the Sharpe ratio is: (expected return − risk-free rate) / expected standard deviation.

Downside Portfolio B = 8.36% − (2 × 10.45%) = −12.54%

Downside Portfolio C = 8.25% − (2 × 10.91%) = −13.57%

Now, we can **eliminate Portfolio C** because its downside risk is too high. A two-standard deviation loss is 13.57% while only −12.54% for Portfolio B.

Therefore, Portfolio B is the most appropriate for the client.

Commom pitfalls to avoid:
1. **Immediate selection of the portfolio with the highest Sharpe ratio.** Portfolio D has the highest Sharpe ratio of 0.649, but cannot be eliminated because it does not meet the liquidity constraint. Remember, only invoke the use of the Sharpe ratio if there is a tie after you have conducted Steps 1 through 3.
2. **Cash allocation is too high.** Even though a portfolio satisfies the client's liquidity constraint, watch for excessive cash. In the example provided, it may also have been possible to eliminate Portfolio C because it has an excessive cash allocation, nearly double of what the client needs. Excess cash unnecessarily drags down portfolio returns.
3. **Misreading the question under pressure.** Recall that the exposure to alternative investments is stated as a "maximum." Under exam pressure and in a hurry, it is possible that some candidates misread the question and interpret it as a "minimum" resulting in the wrong eliminations. The examiners want you to be fast in your calculations and accurate, too.

4. **Reading too much into the numbers in the table.** CFA Institute goes to great lengths to ensure that the questions are of a high quality and are free from errors. It is not your job to question the numbers provided. Accept them. For example, there is enough information in the table for you to compute the Sharpe ratio. However, this only confirms the numbers provided to you. Redoing the calculations slows you down on the exam and increases your chances of not completing it.

How could this be tested?

Take a look at the 2009 exam Q6 (10 minutes; 5% of the morning session).

LESSON 7: MONTE CARLO SIMULATION AND PERSONAL RETIREMENT PLANNING

LOS 10k: Compare Monte Carlo and traditional deterministic approaches to retirement planning and explain the advantages of a Monte Carlo approach. Vol 2, pp 196–199

Monte Carlo Simulation

Monte Carlo simulation uses path-dependent scenarios, developed based on probability distributions, to predict final-stage outcomes. Path dependence means that the outcome for a particular stage depends on what happens in the previous stage. *Deterministic simulation,* by contrast, uses a single variable at each stage rather than a probability distribution. Monte Carlo simulation provides more information about risk than deterministic simulation, often allowing an investor to change controllable variables in response to the risk information provided.

Because a probability distribution can be built around various nodes of the simulation, investors can answer the question "What is the likelihood of earning 7.5 percent after-tax on my investments?" rather than "How much money will I have if I earn 7.5 percent after-tax return on my investments?" as with a deterministic scenario. It is easy to determine the return requirement and develop a deterministic scenario, but Monte Carlo simulation helps answer the better question.

In addition, the sequential nature of the Monte Carlo simulations allows inclusion of various tax consequences created by decisions or additional contributions at each node.

Monte Carlo methods are not, however, a panacea and should be viewed with skepticism (as with any approach):

- Different vendors have various levels of quantitative reliability.
- Past performance may provide a poor estimate of future results.
- Asset class returns don't necessarily reflect after-fee returns from a specific investment in the asset class. In other words, Monte Carlo simulation is best conducted using investment returns, not asset class returns.
- Monte Carlo simulations should be flexible enough to allow investor-specific tax scenarios.

READING 11: TAXES AND PRIVATE WEALTH MANAGEMENT IN A GLOBAL CONTEXT

Time to complete: 2 to 3 hours

Reading Summary: This reading could be tested either in the morning or afternoon session, so be prepared for it either way. The focus of this reading is on the power of tax deferral, a strategy that works best over a long investment horizon. You do not need to know tax codes for any specific country for the CFA Level III exam.

Modern portfolio theory traditionally studied pre-tax investment returns that were subject to risk preferences and other constraints. This makes sense in a tax-exempt framework suitable for institutional investing, but falls short when describing a taxable world. In addition to buying and selling securities and maintaining an appropriate asset allocation, private wealth managers can add value to client accounts by helping them maximize *after-tax* returns.

This lesson will provide you with the tools to:

1. Compare different tax regimes, calculate taxes, and determine how taxes affect after-tax returns and investment risk for various investors and types of accounts;
2. Determine how investor trading behavior, investment horizon, and return impact tax liability; and
3. Explain various tax-minimizing strategies and tax-efficient portfolio optimization.

LESSON 1: OVERVIEW OF GLOBAL INCOME TAX STRUCTURES

TAX STRUCTURES

Governments use taxes to generate revenues for various programs, change opportunity costs to affect behavior (e.g., encourage retirement saving), and perhaps other reasons. Taxes generally take these forms:

- *Income*—How and when different types of income are taxed, including salaries, wages, realized and unrealized capital gains, interest, etc.
- *Consumption*—Taxes collected on intermediate production steps (e.g., value added tax or "VAT"), or in one step from the end user (e.g., sales taxes).
- *Wealth*—Taxes on accumulated financial assets and property, as well as transferring such accumulation to heirs (i.e., inheritance).

Taxes and even tax environments can change over time, so approaches to wealth management should provide a framework for addressing specific tax situations.

Common Structures

Taxing schemes may differentiate between income earned from work (i.e., *ordinary income*) and income earned from investments (i.e., *investment income*, including interest, dividends, capital gains, etc.). Income taxes may take the form of a single tax rate applied to all sources of income (flat tax), or a schedule of graduated marginal rates applied incrementally as income increases (progressive tax).

Example 1-1

Jeremy Bindle earns adjusted gross income (after all deductions) of $100,000 from his employment. He is subject to the following progressive tax rate schedule, which applies to ordinary income:

10% on taxable income from $0 to $8,925, plus

15% on taxable income over $8,925 to $36,250, plus

25% on taxable income over $36,250 to $87,850, plus

28% on taxable income over $87,850 to $183,250

Bindle's income tax liability will be *closest* to:

   A. $19,500

   B. $21,300

   C. $28,100

Solution:

   B. Bindle's tax is:

$$(100,000 - 87,850) \times 0.28 = 3,402.00$$
$$(87,850 - 36,250) \times 0.25 = 12,900.00$$
$$(36,250 - 8,925) \times 0.15 = 4,098.75$$
$$8,925 \times 0.10 = 892.50$$
$$\text{Total} \qquad\qquad\qquad 21,293.25$$

In order to promote certain public policies, tax rates on interest income from municipal projects, hospitals, etc. may be lower. Tax credits may apply to ordinary income or the overall tax bill for such expenses as education, upgrades that improve environmental efficiency, etc. Capital gains taxes may be higher for short-term holding periods (generally less than one year) versus long-term holding periods. In most cases, capital gains tax applies when selling the asset, although in certain jurisdictions, tax may accrue during the asset holding period if the owners change their citizenship status or in the event of intergenerational transfers, like non-spousal inheritance.

Taxes may also be deferred, such as by allowing a deduction for contributions to a retirement account now with tax on the amount withdrawn at some later time, usually upon reaching some minimum age or under exceptional circumstances specified in the tax code.

Income Tax Regimes

Tax structures will generally be considered either flat or progressive, with further categorization based on differences in the tax applied to various components of investment return:

- *Progressive* (most common)—Tax rates generally increase as ordinary income increases. In some jurisdictions, interest and realized short-term gains may be taxed as ordinary income.
- *Heavy dividend tax*—Progressive ordinary income tax rates that include dividends, with lower rates for interest income and capital gains.
- *Heavy capital gains tax* (uncommon)—Progressive ordinary income tax rates that include capital gains, with lower rates for interest and dividends.
- *Heavy interest income tax*—Progressive ordinary income tax rates that include interest, with lower rates for dividends and capital gains.
- *Light capital gains tax* (2nd most common)—Progressive ordinary income tax rates that include interest and dividends, with lower rates for capital gains.

- *Flat and heavy*—Flat tax on ordinary income including dividends and capital gains, with lower rates for interest income.
- *Flat and light*—Flat tax on ordinary income, with lower rates for dividends, capital gains, and interest income.

LESSON 2: AFTER-TAX ACCUMULATIONS AND RETURNS FOR TAXABLE ACCOUNTS

LOS 11b: Determine the effects of different types of taxes and tax regimes on future wealth accumulation. **Vol 2, pp 232–243**

LOS 11c: Explain how investment return and investment horizon affect the tax impact associated with an investment. **Vol 2, pp 232–243**

TAX IMPACTS ON ACCUMULATION

Keep in mind that the wealth manager's primary objective is to maximize his clients' *after-tax* wealth within established constraints. Consider a client whose financial goal is to fund her retirement. The funds she will live on after she stops working will be after-tax dollars. Therefore, in planning her investment strategy, the manager must incorporate the impact of taxes on her expected wealth accumulation.

Recall that investment returns will come in three forms: income, realized gains, and unrealized gains. Since each of these return components may be taxed differently, the manager must incorporate the tax regime into his asset accumulation model. Furthermore, by making tactical choices with respect to taxes, the manager can add value, a concept that is often referred to as tax alpha or tax efficiency.

This section presents different approaches to estimating the tax impact on asset accumulation, given the tax rates and method of applying the tax. We consider two ways of incurring tax liabilities. The first approach applies tax rates to income annually, such that the tax liability is accrued, levied, and paid on a periodic basis. The second method defers, or postpones, the tax liability until some future date.

A Simple Environment

Here we assume several simplifications for the sake of understanding the impact of taxes on investment returns. In this case, we are assuming a flat tax regime.

Annual Accrual with a Single, Uniform Tax Rate

Under a flat tax regime that uses the accrual method for all investment income, a single tax rate is applied to all investment income. The impact on the future asset accumulation can be shown by multiplying the current asset base by the future value interest factor (FVIF). The FVIF can be computed on a pre-tax and after-tax basis.

$$FVIF_{\text{pre-tax}} = \left(1 + r_{\text{pre-tax}}\right)^n$$

$$FVIF_{\text{after-tax}} = \left[1 + r_{\text{pre-tax}}\left(1 - t_i\right)\right]^n$$

TAXES AND PRIVATE WEALTH MANAGEMENT IN A GLOBAL CONTEXT

Where $r_{\text{pre-tax}}$ is the investment return on a pre-tax basis, t_i is the accrual tax rate applied to annual income, and the after-tax return is found by:

$$r_{\text{after-tax}} = r_{\text{pre-tax}}\left(1 - t_i\right)$$

The difference between the pre-tax asset accumulation and the after-tax accumulation is referred to as tax drag, the net loss to income taxes.

Several plain English conclusions about the impact of taxes result from application of this formula:

- The rate of tax drag is greater than the tax rate because compounding amplifies the nominal tax rate's effect;
- Tax drag increases as the pre-tax investment return increases;
- Tax drag increases as the investment horizon increases; and
- Investment return and time horizon have multiplicative effects on tax drag.

Example 2-1

Emmanuelle Rodriguez lives in a jurisdiction with a flat tax of 20 percent on all income as it is earned. Her initial portfolio of GBP 250,000 earns 10 percent annually. The value of her portfolio at the end of 15 years will be *closest* to:

    A. 511,205

    B. 793,042

    C. 849,936

Solution:

    B. Rodriguez's portfolio will have an after-tax value after 15 years of:

$$V_{15} = 250{,}000 \times [1 + 0.10(1 - 0.20)]^{15} = 793{,}042$$

Deferral Method with a Single, Uniform Tax Rate

Most tax regimes defer capital gains taxes until they are realized. For example, a non-dividend paying stock would owe no taxes until it is sold and a capital gain is realized. There are a couple of ways to represent this mathematically, but both methods recognize there is no tax on the original investment when returned to the investor. The simplest method to represent this is:

$$FVIF = \left(1 + r_{CG}\right)^n\left(1 - t_{CG}\right) + t_{CG}$$

The leftmost term represents the entire return of the investment after taxes have been removed, where the rightmost term essentially adds the tax on the initial investment amount, assuming that to be full cost basis (V_0 = cost basis).

The proportionate tax drag under a deferral structure is the same as the tax rate, unlike the higher tax drag associated with the accrual method. Even if the rate is the same in accrual and deferral, the deferral approach has an after-tax accumulation advantage for the investor.

Example 2-2

Emmanuelle Rodriguez lives in a jurisdiction with a 20% flat tax on all types of income. Her initial portfolio of GBP 250,000 grows 10% annually, all of which comes from unrealized capital gains. The after-tax value of her portfolio if disposed of at the end of 15 years will be *closest* to:

    A. 679,949

    B. 875,450

    C. 885,450

Solution:

    C. Rodriguez's portfolio will have an after-tax value after 15 years of:

$$V_{15} = 250,000 \times [(1 + 0.10)^{15}(1 - 0.20) + 0.20] = 885,450$$

Taxable Gains When the Cost Basis Differs From Current Value

The *cost basis* of an asset is the starting value from which the gain or loss for tax purposes is determined. It is usually, but not always, equal to the original cost of acquiring the asset. In the previous example, the capital gain was calculated using the current value of the asset (V_0), which effectively assumes that it was purchased in the current period. The cost basis may differ from the current value if it was purchased in a preceding period. For example, an investor might have purchased the asset three years ago for $5,000, but today it is worth $7,500. If the asset were sold today, it would have an embedded gain of $2,500 that would be subject to tax.

The cost basis might also be changed from the original purchase price in the case of inheritance or through a corporate merger. Generally, investors want the cost basis to be as high as possible in order to minimize the capital gain and, thus, the capital gains tax, which decreases as the cost basis increases.

$$\text{Taxable gain} = V_T - \text{Cost basis}$$

The implication is that newly invested capital has a cost basis equal to the investment value, while other assets may have an embedded capital gain that creates a tax burden if the asset were sold today. A future value for an asset with taxable basis (B) expressed as a proportion of current value could be expressed mathematically as:

$$FVIF_{\text{Capital gain}} = (1 + r_{\text{pre-tax}})^n (1 - t_{CG}) + t_{CG}B$$

where:

$$B = \frac{\text{Cost basis}}{V_0}$$

The left side of the expression applies the gains tax rate to the entire accumulation, while the right side adds back the tax applied to the cost basis.

Example 2-3

Rhonda Jenkins lives in a jurisdiction with a 23 percent capital gains tax rate. She owns a non-dividend paying stock that is currently valued at €60,000. However, the recognized cost basis of the holding is €54,000. If the stock is expected to appreciate by 10 percent each year, the after-tax value of her holding if disposed of at the end of 5 years will be *closest* to:

A. €74,406

B. €82,151

C. €86,826

Solution:

C. The holding will have an after-tax value after 5 years of:

$$V_5 = €60,000 \times FVIF = €60,000 \times [(1 + 0.10)^5(1 - 0.23) + 0.23(0.90)]$$
$$= €86,825.56$$

Thus, when a portfolio has a lower cost basis than current market value at the beginning of the accumulation period, the capital gains tax liability will be greater than if the portfolio were acquired at market value on the first day of the accumulation period. Having a basis less than cost could alternatively be thought of as earning a gain subject to gains tax that was excluded with a full cost basis asset.

Wealth Tax Regimes

A wealth tax is applied to the value of assets, not just their derived income or gains. Taxes on accumulated wealth may apply only to real property, to accumulated assets over some threshold, or to everything. For accumulations taxed annually, the future value index factor formula is:

$$FVIF_{\text{Wealth tax}} = \left[\left(1 + r_{\text{pre-tax}}\right)\left(1 - t_W\right) \right]^n$$

Wealth tax rates will tend to be lower than annual accrual income tax rates, but are applied to a much larger asset base rather than just the dividend and income earnings or the gain on the investment. Wealth taxes have a greater effect on the growth when the accumulation has a low return because the tax represents a greater percentage of the return. *In fact, in years where the wealth tax rate is higher than the asset return, principal will erode.* Wealth taxes, like accrual and deferred taxes, also take a larger percentage of the gain as the time horizon increases.

Example 2-4

Sarah Chen lives in a jurisdiction with a 2% annual wealth tax on the value of financial assets. Her initial portfolio of CHF 750,000 is expected to grow at a 6% annual return. The after-tax value of her portfolio if disposed of at the end of 15 years will be *closest* to:

    A. CHF 969,358

    B. CHF 1,327,518

    C. CHF 2,171,049

Solution:

    B. The portfolio will have an after-tax value after 15 years of:

$$V_{15} = 750,000 \times FVIF_{WT} = 750,000 \times [(1 + 0.06)(1 - 0.02)]^{15} = 1,327,518$$

Complex Tax Environments

Having looked at simple tax structures, we now recognize that investors may have more than one source of return from their investments (interest, dividends, realized, and unrealized gains), each of which might be taxed at a different rate or deferred. If we know the proportions (P_i) of total pre-tax return r_T represented by each source, including the proportion of realized capital gain P_{RCG}, we can integrate the tax effects into a single model of the *effective after-tax return* (r^*) for investment income and realized capital gains:

$$r^* = r_T \left(1 - P_I t_I - P_D t_D - P_{RCG} t_{CG}\right)$$

Example 2-5

Elrud Schmidt's portfolio earns an overall pre-tax return of 10 percent. It generates 20 percent of this return from dividends, 30 percent from interest, and 50 percent from realized capital gains. The taxes on each type of return are 20%, 30%, and 15%, respectively. The portfolio's expected effective after-tax return from realized sources will be *closest* to:

    A. 6%

    B. 8%

    C. 9%

Solution:

    B. Schmidt's effective after-tax return on the portfolio is:

$$r^* = 0.10[1 - (0.20)(0.20) - (0.30)(0.30) - (0.50)(0.15)] = 0.0795$$

Unrealized capital gains, which will eventually be taxed upon selling the asset, remain excluded from the effective after-tax return. In order to incorporate those future taxes on unrealized gains, an *effective capital gains tax rate* (T^*) applicable to the unrealized capital gain must be calculated by applying the capital gains tax rate (t_{CG}) to the proportion of unrealized gain:

$$T^* = t_{CG}\left(\frac{1 - P_I - P_D - P_{RCG}}{1 - P_I t - P_D T_D - P_{RCG} t_{CG}}\right)$$

The future value multiplier under this blended tax regime then becomes:

$$FVIF_{\text{after-tax}} = (1 + r^*)^n (1 - T^*) + T^* - t_{CG}(1 - B)$$

Example 2-6

Ted Barsman's portfolio has a cost basis and current value of $50,000. He has prepared the following summary information:

	% Return Distribution (P_i)	Tax Rate (t_i)
Income	10%	30%
Dividends	20%	15%
Realized capital gains	40%	20%
Investment horizon	5 years	
Average annual return	7.5%	

The expected after-tax accumulation in five years will be *closest* to:

A. $65,000

B. $67,000

C. $78,000

Solution:

B. The effective after-tax return (excluding unrealized gains) is:

$$r^* = r_T \left(1 - P_I t_I - P_D t_D - P_{RCG} t_{CG}\right)$$
$$= 0.075 \left[1 - 0.10(0.30) - 0.20(0.15) - 0.40(0.20)\right] = 0.0645$$

The effective tax on unrealized capital gains is:

$$T^* = t_{CG}\left(\frac{1 - P_I - P_D - P_{RCG}}{1 - P_I t - P_D T_D - P_{RCG} t_{CG}}\right)$$
$$= 0.20(0.30 / 0.86) = 0.06977$$

The after-tax accumulation after 5 years will be:

$$FVIF = (1 + r^*)^n (1 - T^*) + T^* - t_{CG}(1 - B)$$
$$(1 + 0.0645)^5 (1 - 0.06977) + 0.06977 - 0.20(1 - 1) = 1.34$$
$$\$50,000(1.34) = \$67,064$$

ACCRUAL EQUIVALENTS

The different types of return, each potentially subject to a different tax, can complicate an understanding of how taxes affect the portfolio. An *accrual equivalent* after-tax return can help us to appreciate the tax effects by showing the tax-free return required to earn the same after-tax accumulation as the taxable portfolio. The proportionate tax drag on the portfolio is equal to the difference between the accrual equivalent tax-free return and the taxable return. Alternatively, we could look at the *accrual equivalent tax rate* that equates the tax-free portfolio to the taxable portfolio.

Accrual Equivalent Return

The *accrual equivalent return* (r_{AE}) is the return required to grow the current portfolio value (V_0) to the after-tax portfolio value at time period n, (V_n):

$$V_n = V_0 \left(1 + r_{AE}\right)^n$$
$$r_{AE} = \sqrt[n]{\frac{V_n}{V_0}} - 1$$

The accrual equivalent return will be less than the annual return after taxes because it considers the deferred tax on gains realized at the end of the holding period. It will approach the pre-tax return value as more tax is deferred or as the time horizon increases, highlighting the importance of deferring taxes.

Example 2-7

Emmanuelle Rodriguez lives in a jurisdiction with a 20% flat tax on all types of income. Her initial portfolio of GBP 250,000 grows 10% annually, all of which comes from unrealized capital gains. Her investment horizon is 15 years. Rodriguez would be equally well off by finding a tax-free investment earning accrual equivalent return *closest* to:

A. 6.8%

B. 8.8%

C. 28.8%

Solution:

B. Rodriguez's expected wealth in 15 years is:

$$V_{15} = 250{,}000[(1 + 0.10)^{15}(1 - 0.20) + 0.20] = 885{,}449.63$$

Accrual equivalent return is:

$$r_{AE} = \sqrt[15]{\frac{885{,}449.63}{250{,}000}} - 1 = 0.08796$$

Accrual Equivalent Tax Rates

The *accrual equivalent tax rate* hypothetically equates the pre-tax return (r) with the accrual equivalent return r_{AE}:

$$r_{AE} = r(1 - T_{AE})$$

$$T_{AE} = 1 - \frac{r_{AE}}{r}$$

The accrual equivalent tax rate will be lower when more of the portfolio is in tax-favored instruments than heavily taxed assets. A *tax-efficient portfolio* takes advantage of these favorable tax methods, including deferred tax on long-term gains.

The accrual equivalent tax rate is a measure of tax drag and can be used to compare the efficiency of asset classes or management styles, as well as the impact of different holding periods. Accrual equivalent tax rates may also be useful in helping clients understand how changes in their circumstances or statutory rates will affect after-tax returns.

Example 2-8

Bessie Smith has a portfolio earning 10% annually and is subject to tax on income from all sources at a flat rate of 20%. This portfolio achieves an accrual equivalent rate of 8.796%. Smith's accrual equivalent tax rate will be *closest* to:

    A. 12.0%

    B. 12.4%

    C. 13.7%

Solution:

    A. Smith's accrual equivalent tax rate is:

$$T_{AE} = 1 - \frac{0.08796}{0.10} = 0.1204$$

LESSON 3: TYPES OF INVESTMENT ACCOUNTS AND TAXES AND INVESTMENT RISK

LOS 11d: Discuss the tax profiles of different types of investment accounts and explain their impact on after-tax returns and future accumulations. Vol 2, pp 245–250

TYPES OF INVESTMENT ACCOUNTS

Governments generally tax investment accounts according to three schemes:

1. *Fully taxable*—All investment earnings are subject to taxes at one point or another.
2. *Deferred tax*—Investments are made with pre-tax income (reducing current tax liability) but withdrawals are taxed. *Traditional Individual Retirement Accounts* (IRAs) in the U.S. fall into this category.
3. *Deferred non-taxable withdrawal*—Investments are made with after-tax dollars, but the principal and returns may be withdrawn tax free. In the U.S., *Roth Individual Retirement Accounts* fall into this category.

Tax-Deferred Accounts

Tax-deferred accounts (TDAs) are taxed with the same structure applicable to zero-cost-basis investments with all returns taxed similar to capital gains:

$$FVIF_{TDA} = \left(1 + r_{CG}\right)^n \left(1 - t_{CG}\right) + t_{CG} \cdot B$$

Note that the rightmost term from the capital gains discussion disappears when investments have zero cost basis.

Tax-Exempt Accounts

Tax-exempt accounts (TEAs) are never taxed, compounding at their pre-tax returns:

$$FVIF_{TEA} = (1+r)^n$$

Assuming equal returns, any type of investment in a tax-exempt account will have greater asset accumulation at the end of the holding period than a taxable account. Because the tax authority owns the deferred tax, the after-tax value of a TDA equals the same value in a tax-exempt account multiplied by $(1 - t)$:

$$FVIF_{TDA} = FVIF_{TEA}(1-t)$$

Example 3-1

Phillip Sandoval is subject to tax on all income at a flat rate of 15%. Sandoval has $100,000 invested in three different types of accounts, each with a 15-year investment horizon, and a 7.5% annual pre-tax return. Which account will have the highest value after liquidation at the end of the investment horizon?

    A.   Tax-exempt account.

    B.   Growth-only account.

    C.   Tax-deferred account.

Solution:

    A.   The tax-exempt account will have the greatest value at the end of the investment horizon:

$$FVIF_{TEA} = (1+r)^n = (1+0.075)^{15} = 2.96$$
$$FVIF_{TEA} = FVIF_{TEA}(1-t) = 2.96(1-0.15) = 2.52$$
$$FVIF_{CG} = (1+r)^n(1-t_{CG})+t_{CG} = (1+0.075)^{15}(1-0.15)+0.15 = 2.67$$

    Each of these FVIF is then multiplied by the initial amount of $100,000 to determine the final portfolio value after liquidation and taxes, if applicable.

Asset Allocation and Taxes

An investor with a particular dollar figure in mind at the end of an investment horizon should consider how the taxability of the accounts could potentially affect asset allocation during the accumulation period. In the simple case of an investor with both a TDA and a TEA, the TDA will cause the after-tax equity exposure of the combined accounts to be less than the pre-tax equity exposure.

Account Choice

Although money invested in a TEA always has a higher after-tax value at the end of an investment horizon than does a similarly-earning TDA, this ignores the potential tax deduction for money invested into the TDA (as with the traditional IRA in the U.S.), where a TEA may be invested with after-tax dollars (as with the Roth IRA in the U.S.).

Because the TEA uses already-taxed dollars, the equation that considers the pre-investment taxation becomes:

$$V_n = V_0(1 - t_0)(1 + r)^n$$

Compare that to the future value of a pre-tax investment in a TDA:

$$V_n = V_0(1 + r)^n(1 - t_n)$$

The TEA (populated with after-tax dollars) and TDA (populated with pre-tax dollars) provide *exactly* the same value at the end of the time horizon *assuming tax rates remain constant!* Clearly, the value at the end of the time horizon will be less for the TDA if tax rates increase, so it may be best to pay the tax now rather than later. Conversely, a falling tax rate environment would suggest paying the tax later rather than now. However, contribution limits on such a program mean that it would be better to invest the maximum amount in the TEA rather than the TDA, because the TEA allows a greater *after-tax* contribution to the investment account, unless the expected tax rate differential suggests otherwise.

Example 3-2

A client wishes to know whether she should allocate $5,500 of income to either a tax-exempt account funded with after-tax dollars or a tax-deferred account funded with pre-tax dollars. The return will be 7% in either account. Her investment horizon is 20 years. The client pays tax at a 25% rate now, but her advisor expects taxes to change over time. What future tax rate will provide the same future value for the Traditional IRA as will be provided by the Roth IRA?

    A.   Exactly 25%.

    B.   Below 25%.

    C.   Above 25%.

> **Solution:**
>
> A. The return for either account will be the same if taxes stay the same. If taxes decrease, the TDA will provide a greater future value. If taxes increase, the TEA will provide a greater future value. The value formula for a tax exempt account is:
>
> $$V_n = V_0(1 - t_0)(1 + r)^n$$
>
> The value formula for a tax-deferred account is:
>
> $$V_n = V_0(1 + r)^n(1 - t_n)$$

LOS 11e: Explain how taxes affect investment risk. Vol 2, pp 250–251

TAX EFFECTS ON INVESTMENT RISK

Whenever it taxes periodic investment returns, the government shares in both the investment return and investment risk commensurate with the tax rate. The investor's after-tax risk, as measured by the standard deviation of return, is:

$$\sigma_{AT} = \sigma(1 - t)$$

This assumes all investment losses can offset returns in the year incurred, and the tax rate (t) is the ordinary rate for all investment returns. In this way, taxes paid annually reduce the portfolio's volatility from the investor's perspective. This has an implication for optimizing asset allocation. Because returns within TEAs and TDAs are not taxed during the accumulation period, investors bear all the risk of those accounts. Therefore, the tax on TDA withdrawals does not affect the return on investments within the TDA for asset allocation purposes.

The method of calculating portfolio standard deviation still applies, although different tax rates may apply to the standard deviation of each asset class. The point that taxes reduce risk across the portfolio still applies regardless of correlations between or among asset classes.

LESSON 4: IMPLICATIONS FOR WEALTH MANAGEMENT

LOS 11f: Discuss the relation between after-tax returns and different types of investor trading behavior. Vol 2, pp 251–260

LOS 11g: Explain the benefits of tax loss harvesting and highest-in/first-out (HIFO) tax lot accounting. Vol 2, pp 251–260

WEALTH MANAGEMENT IMPLICATIONS

Tax alpha describes preserving potential return from shrinkage due to taxes. Because investors can only spend the after-tax return from a portfolio, advisors can potentially add significant value by making tax-informed investment decisions.

Account Type

Governments often place limits on tax-exempt or tax-deferred accounts in order to prevent high-net worth (HNW) investors from avoiding tax altogether. Therefore, such investors typically have several different types of accounts in which they hold their assets, *asset locations*. The asset location decision is distinct from the asset allocation decision, although the tax structure has implications for both.

Individual investors may hold investments subject to greater tax burden in tax-exempt accounts and then round out their asset allocation by holding investments subject to lighter tax burden in taxable accounts. Black and Tepper theorized that tax-exempt or tax-deferred locations, such as a pension fund, might be completely populated with investments having greater tax liability against the returns. Lightly-taxed assets could be held outside the pension fund and any asset allocation difference from excessive allocation to the non-taxable location could be offset by a short position outside that location. The magnitude of the short position would to some extent depend on the tax rate.

The following illustration assumes the simple example of the Black and Tepper approach in which the investor with a $200,000 portfolio should have a 60% bond and 40% equity allocation, but instead has 75% in a TDA populated with bonds and 25% in a taxable account populated with stocks.

Exhibit 4-1: Black and Tepper Approach (Pre-Tax Values)

Account Type	Asset Class	Existing Market Value	Existing Allocation %	Asset Class	Target Market Value	Target Allocation %
TDA	Bond	150,000	75	Bond	150,000	75
				Short Bond	(30,000)	(15)
Taxable	Stock	50,000	25	Stock	80,000	40
Total		200,000	100		200,000	100

Portfolio managers should make the asset location and asset allocation decisions jointly to maximize overall portfolio return after any changes, keeping in mind that changing an asset's location can create a taxable event or may change the after-tax asset allocation. There is also the additional problem of a difference in borrowing and lending rates to which most investors have access and at least a portion of the gain from reducing taxes will be consumed by this rate difference. Some investors have an aversion to financing any portion of their portfolio with debt. Finally, some types of investors, like mutual funds, may be restricted from or limited in the amount of borrowing they may do against the portfolio, especially in a TDA, and some jurisdictions present taxpayers with penalties for withdrawal prior to a certain age or within a certain time frame.

Investors may be forced to liquidate assets in the TDA if the asset value declines substantially in the taxable account. In such a case, and where the investor is limited in borrowing for the taxable account, it would be advisable to achieve the allocation based on a combination of remaining funds in the taxable account and some combination of stocks and bonds in the TDA.

Asset location becomes less important when investment returns, including unrealized capital gains or imputed interest on discount bonds, are taxed annually. Also, target market values should be considered in the context of portfolio management style; e.g., high turnover will result in greater tax liability. Finally, assets held for short-term liquidity purposes or as part of a pyramid of assets may not be appropriate to reallocate based on their taxation.

Trading Behavior

Four different styles of trading behavior may also influence the taxability of accounts:

1. *Traders*—Realize all gains as taxable income. This may erode the benefits of capital gains and make the return taxable similar to bond interest income.
2. *Active investors*—May receive favorable tax treatment if they observe holding periods for long-term capital gains (if applicable in their tax regime).
3. *Passive investors*—Passively buy and hold stocks and may benefit from holding non-dividend paying securities.
4. *Exempt investors*—Buy and hold stocks, or trade stocks, but are not subject to the tax on gains.

Consider in Exhibit 4-2 the case of these four different investors in a tax regime taxing ordinary income (including short-term capital gains) at 35% and long-term capital gains (i.e., after a one-year holding horizon) at 20%, each with $100 to invest and earning 7% annually on the investment over a 20-year horizon:

Exhibit 4-2: Accumulation by Investor Type

Type	Calculation	Future Accumulation	Accrual Equivalent Return	Accrual Equivalent Tax Rate
Trader	$100 [1 + 0.07(1 - 0.35)]^{20}$	243.49	4.55%	35.0%
Active Investor	$100 [1 + 0.07(1 - 0.20)]^{20}$	297.36	5.60%	20.0%
Passive Investor	$100 [(1 + 0.07)^{20}(1 - 0.20) + 0.20]$	317.36	5.94%	15.1%
Exempt Investor	$100 (1 + 0.07)^{20}$	386.97	7.00%	0%

All else being equal, the trader accumulates far less than the tax-exempt investor. Therefore, traders must earn higher pre-tax alpha to offset the tax drag of active management, and locating assets in TDAs and taxable accounts cannot overcome highly tax inefficient strategies or those with negative pre-tax alpha.

Tax Loss Harvesting

Managers can create value for investors by trading out of losing positions in order to offset gains on other securities in a process known as tax loss harvesting. Jurisdictions may only allow current period losses to the extent of realized gains, but may allow excess losses to be carried forward to offset gains in future periods. Investors should be aware that some jurisdictions prevent investors from repurchasing securities sold at a loss, at least for some period of time.

Selling a security at a loss simply to repurchase it or a similar security at a new basis may set up the possibility of equal or greater capital gain in some future period. At best, tax loss harvesting defers tax liabilities rather than eliminates them. However, taxes saved in the current year may be reinvested for additional cumulative gains.

Example 4-1

Evan Drew has $100,000 worth of capital gains derived from assets held in a taxable account. He has assets with unrecognized capital losses of $80,000 that may be liquidated and similar assets repurchased with identical returns. If the capital gains tax rate is 20%, what is Drew's gains tax liability if he offsets the gains by recognizing the losses?

   A. $4,000

   B. $16,000

   C. $20,000

Solution:

   A.   Drew's tax liability will be $(100{,}000 - 80{,}000)(0.20) = \$4{,}000$.

Investors who sell part of a position in a particular security may also save taxes if they are allowed to calculate the gains tax due on that portion of the position with the greatest cost basis, effectively minimizing the gain from the sale in the current period. This often occurs when investors have positions with securities purchased at different times. However, a greater liability will be due on the remaining portion of the position as the result of retaining the lower basis securities.

Investors will realize higher tax benefits from loss harvesting in the early years and declining benefits as deferred gains are realized and taxed, unless they reside in a taxing jurisdiction expected to increase tax rates. Market participants may also benefit from selling low basis (i.e., "high gain") stock if the tax rate is low compared with expected future rates.

Holding Period

Active management can be hard to justify when the tax on short-term gains significantly exceeds the tax on long-term gains. While potential tax benefits are important, selling should also depend on the relative attractiveness of holding the current investment. However, managers must deliver quite a bit of timing alpha to overcome the effects of tax alpha. This can be measured as a ratio of future accumulations for two investments, one at a long-term capital gains rate and the other at a short-term capital gains rate for the same return over the same period:

$$\frac{V_{LTG}}{V_{STG}} = \frac{\left[1 + r\left(1 - t_{LTG}\right)\right]^n}{\left[1 + r\left(1 - t_{STG}\right)\right]^n}$$

The ratio clearly shows that the ratio and, therefore, the value of long-term gains will increase as the return, the short-term vs. long-term tax rate difference, and the holding period increase. Penalties from realizing short-term gains can also be thought of as the equivalent pre-tax return *PTR* required to offset the difference in gains tax:

$$PTR_{STG} = \frac{ATR_{LTG}}{1-t_{STG}} = r\left(\frac{1-t_{LTG}}{1-t_{STG}}\right)$$

In other words, investors can determine the portion of return kept from long-term vs. short-term gains, and this difference becomes more important as the holding period increases.

Example 4-2

Evan Drew resides in a tax jurisdiction with a 40% tax on short-term capital gains and 20% tax on long-term capital gains. Drew will have a 12% pre-tax return if he waits to sell an asset as a long-term gain. What pre-tax return will Drew require to sell that same asset for a short-term gain?

    A. 9%

    B. 12%

    C. 16%

Solution:

    C. Drew will require a pre-tax return in a short-term gain situation of:

$$PTR_{STG} = \frac{ATR_{LTG}}{1-t_{STG}} = 0.12\left(\frac{1-0.20}{1-0.40}\right) = 0.16$$

Mean-Variance Optimization

An asset class in a pre-tax context is quite different from one in an after-tax environment, essentially changing the Sharpe ratio for the asset because it changes both the return and the risk of the asset. Therefore, an investor with investments in two asset classes across two taxing environments (e.g., TDA and taxable) essentially has four asset classes that must be optimized into a portfolio. Optimizing such a portfolio simply involves using equivalent annual returns rather than pre-tax returns and after-tax rather than pre-tax standard deviations.

Certain constraints involve limiting immediate reallocation in the TDA to funds already in the TDA, such as to avoid contribution limit violations or early withdrawal penalties. Other limitations may involve the type of assets allowable by the taxing jurisdiction in the TDA.

READING 12: ESTATE PLANNING IN A GLOBAL CONTEXT

Time to complete: 2 to 3 hours

Reading Summary: Efficient estate planning starts at an early age for high net worth investors. You will learn that gifting money over an investor's lifetime helps to reduce the size of a taxable estate at death. As in taxes, you are not responsible for knowing specific tax rates related to gifting or estates for any particular country.

High net worth individuals (HNWIs) often have family and financial interests in multiple legal and tax jurisdictions, which presents an opportunity for wealth managers to add value to the relationship by coordinating professional responses to estate planning and inheritance tax issues spanning these jurisdictions. While the specifics of estate planning should be left to experts within a jurisdiction, the wealth advisor can communicate the need for such services to clients and develop frameworks to help address those needs.

This lesson will provide you with the tools to:

1. Evaluate a client's jurisdiction for estate tax purposes;
2. Evaluate and explain basic estate planning considerations and the strategies designed to address them; and
3. Evaluate a client's potential tax liability based on the method employed in the applicable jurisdiction(s).

LOS 12a: Discuss the purpose of estate planning and explain the basic concepts of domestic estate planning, including estates, wills, and probate. Vol 2, pp 273–276

LESSON 1: DOMESTIC ESTATE PLANNING: SOME BASIC CONCEPTS

Estate planning is the process of establishing a plan for transferring or disposing of an *estate* (i.e., all of the property one owns or controls) during one's remaining life or afterward. It may also involve powers of attorney during periods of incapacitation, medical instructions, and burial preferences.

Estates, Wills, and Probate

An estate for an HNWI will often include:

- *Financial assets*—Bank accounts, financial instruments such as stocks and bonds, and privately held business interests;
- *Immovable property*—Real estate, timber rights, etc.;
- *Intellectual property*—Patents or royalty income; and
- *Personal assets*—Cars, boats, clothing, artwork, and other collectibles.

Estates might exclude portions of property gifted *inter vivos* (i.e., during the giver's life) or transferred to a trust. The *settlor* of a trust (person who establishes and transfers assets) may, depending on jurisdiction, retain liability for tax on the trust assets even though the trustee retains legal ownership.

A *testator* will often author a *will* (i.e., testament) outlining how property will transfer to the beneficiaries. Assets of a *decedent* (person who has died) without a valid will (i.e., *intestate)* are subject to distribution according to prevailing law. Therefore, a will goes through *probate* to determine its authenticity. The probate process, however, can delay transfer of assets, expose family secrets, and create large fees against the estate, especially if challenged. Some assets (e.g., retirement accounts, life insurance) avoid probate by naming a beneficiary, while other assets (e.g., real estate) accomplish this through forms of ownership (e.g., joint tenancy with rights of survivorship, tenancy in common, etc.).

Living trusts allow the settler of the trust to retain ownership over the assets in the trust or confer ownership to a different trustee during life or at death. The living trust may continue after the settlor's death. Income from this type of arrangement, however, remains the settlor's responsibility for tax purposes, but avoids the delay, potential publicity, and expenses associated with probating a will.

Legal Systems

Civil law, the deductive reasoning used in most countries, applies abstract rules and concepts to specific cases while common law, the deductive reasoning used in the U.S. and U.K., abstracts rules and concepts from outcomes of specific cases. In other words, civil law relies on law to adjudicate cases while common law relies on outcomes of cases to establish or clarify law.

Common law jurisdictions typically allow the testator significant judgment in the disposition of assets after death. Civil law jurisdictions often place restrictions on how the testator disposes of property and may not allow a trust, which is a feature of common law.

Civil law also typically features *forced heirship rules*, in which children of the decedent have a right to some share of the estate regardless of estrangement or conception outside of marriage. Some HNWIs may attempt to circumvent such rules by establishing offshore trusts or *inter vivos gifting*. Some jurisdictions, however, allow heirs to claw back gifts or other portions of the estate if remaining assets are not sufficient to cover the heir's claim.

Spouses also have heirship rights under civil law, and separate marital property rights depending on the jurisdiction's regime:

- *Community property*—Property acquired or received after marriage creates an indivisible half-interest for each partner. Property acquired prior to the marriage remains as separate property. Upon death, one half of the decedent's community property passes to the surviving spouse with the remainder transferred according to the provisions of a will.
- *Separate property*—Each partner may own or control property as an individual, subject to heirship and other jurisdictional rules.

In many civil law countries, partners may elect which regime applies to their property. In other regimes, forced heirship rules apply to both separate and community property owned by the decedent.

Example 1-1

Astrid Pedersen lives in a community property regime in which a spouse is entitled to one-half the community property at the death of the other spouse. Prior to their marriage, her husband received a gift of shares valued as of his death at $1.5 million that will be considered separate property. The total estate was valued at $7.5 million as of his death. Forced heirship rules require that the surviving spouse receive at least one-quarter of the total estate, and the children split at least one-quarter of the estate. How much will Astrid's husband be able to leave to his favorite charity?

- A. $1.875m
- B. $2.625m
- C. $4.875m

Solution:

B. Astrid will be entitled to one-half the community property (CP) or one-quarter of the entire estate under forced heirship rules (FHR), whichever is greater. The children will be entitled to one-quarter of the entire estate under FHR. The husband's portion available to donate to the Libertarian think tank is:

$7.500	Total estate
($3.000)	Astrid CP [0.5 × ($7.5 – $1.5)]
($1.875)	Children FHR [0.25 × $7.5]
$4.875	Total to Astrid and children
$2.625	Available to donate

LOS 12b: Explain the two principal forms of wealth transfer taxes and discuss effects of important non-tax issues, such as legal system, forced heirship, and marital property regime. Vol 2, pp 276–278

Wealth Transfer Taxes

Taxing jurisdictions may tax:

- *Income*—Often income taxes, with differentiation for active/passive or labor/ investment income.
- *Spending*—Usually sales taxes, although excise taxes may apply to the purchased item and are often not observable in the price.
- *Wealth*—May be levied against the entire base, or the net worth (assets – liabilities) balance.
- *Wealth transfer*—Inter vivos (during life) transfers or testamentary (after death) transfers subject to *inheritance taxes*. Wealth transfer taxes may provide a statutory allowance not subject to tax, be flat, or be progressive (scaled based on size), etc.

Example 1-2

Richard Thornby died with an estate worth €1.2 million. The first €350,000 will not be subject to estate taxes (statutory allowance) and may be distributed as the decedent wishes. The remainder will be subject to 30 percent tax, with the after-tax amount to be distributed as the decedent wishes. Thornby's estate will have a total value to heirs closest to:

A. €595,000

B. €840,000

C. €945,000

Solution:

C. The initial amount of €350,000 will go to heirs. The heirs will keep 70% of the remaining €850,000 (€1,200,000 – €350,000) or €595,000 (€850,000 × 0.70). The total passed to heirs will be €945,000 (€350,000 + €595,000).

LESSON 2: CORE CAPITAL AND EXCESS CAPITAL

LOS 12c: Determine a family's core capital and excess capital, based on mortality probabilities and Monte Carlo analysis. **Vol 2, pp 278–288**

EXCESS CAPITAL

Transferring wealth as desired may be impossible for most estate planning clients as the result of low resources, the growing number of heirs, various types of *inter vivos* and testamentary transfer taxes, or some combination of challenges. An estate plan must start with the idea of how much can be passed to heirs or otherwise gifted, and this will be based on the desires of the decedent and the spending needs of the first generation to receive the wealth transfer.

One method of reaching a conclusion on wealth begins with netting liabilities against the total of explicit assets (e.g., stocks, bonds, business value, real estate, etc.) and implicit assets (i.e., *human capital* comprised of the present value of net employment income, the present value of expected pension benefits, etc.). The liabilities component should include explicit liabilities (e.g., mortgage loan debt, margin account debt, credit card debt, etc.) and implicit liabilities such as the present value of the client's life spending goals. The net of liabilities against assets could be described as *net present value of wealth*.

The client's *core capital* will be required to fund the client's existing or aspirational lifestyle and maintain a reserve for unexpected expenses. The amount remaining after subtracting core capital from the net present value of wealth is known as *excess capital*, which may be transferred by the client without affecting lifestyle goals.

Exhibit 2-1: Net Present Value of Wealth

Assets
  Real estate
  Financial assets
  Other investments
  Life insurance and other assets
  PV net employment capital (also known as human capital)
    Total assets
Liabilities
  Credit card and short-term debt
  Brokerage margin account debt
  Mortgages
  PV of educational expenses
  PV of current lifestyle costs
  PV of incremental (aspirational) lifestyle costs
  Retirement
    Total liabilities
    Excess capital

Mortality Tables

Core and excess capital estimates are subject to many risks not discussed above. For example, inflation may increase, market cycles may erode capital when it is most needed, etc. One of the greatest client risks is outliving assets projected to sustain a desired lifestyle. Life expectancy and mortality are often assumed or are averages of current life expectancy.

An alternative approach estimates capital needs as the amount of an expected cash outflow based on *survival probability* (i.e., probability of being alive to need it at that particular time). This becomes a joint probability in the event more than one person will be alive to need the capital at that time.

$$\text{Liability}_0 = \sum_{t=0}^{n} \frac{\text{Expected spending}}{(1+r)^t}$$

$$= \sum_{t=0}^{n} \frac{p(\text{Survival}_t) \times \text{Amount}_t}{(1+r)^t}$$

For cases where more than one client requires the capital, the joint probability calculation is:

$$p(\text{Survival}_{t,C1,C2}) = p(C_1) + p(C_2) - p(C_1)p(C_2)$$

Exhibit 2-2 provides a brief example for a couple, age 91 and 90, assuming spending this year of $250,000 and arbitrary 3% real growth in spending, discounted at the 3.5% real risk-free rate to determine the present value. Note that inflation is not considered in the present value calculation because it was not included in the spending increase. In reality, the forecast spending for a particular year would be substituted for this projected spending estimate. Additionally, updated probabilities would be required as the plan rolls forward each year because, for example, at age 79 the client's chances of making it to age 81 depend on whether they live to be 80.

Exhibit 2-2: Core Capital Requirement

Year	Client 1		Client 2		P(joint)	Annual Spending	Expected Spending	Discounted Value
	Age	p(C1)	Age	p(C2)				
1	91	0.2414	90	0.2912	0.4623	250,000	115,576	111,668
2	92	0.1968	91	0.2414	0.3907	257,500	100,603	93,914
3	93	0.1576	92	0.1968	0.3234	265,225	85,770	77,359
4	94	0.1239	93	0.1576	0.2620	273,182	71,566	62,366
5	95	0.0955	94	0.1239	0.2076	281,377	58,405	49,175
6	96	0.0720	95	0.0955	0.1606	289,819	46,552	37,870
7	97	0.0532	96	0.0720	0.1214	298,513	36,230	28,477
8	98	0.0373	97	0.0532	0.0885	307,468	27,216	20,668
9	99	0.0262	98	0.0373	0.0625	316,693	19,800	14,528
10	100	0.0180	99	0.0262	0.0437	326,193	14,264	10,112
11	101	0.0000	100	0.0180	0.0180	335,979	6,048	4,142
					Core capital requirement			510,280

Decreased annual spending should be considered when one of the clients dies. One estimate suggests that a surviving member of a couple may be able to maintain the same lifestyle at 62.5% of the spending required for the couple. A more conservative forecast for the core capital requirement might be to assume both clients live throughout the forecast horizon and discount the entire amount of annual spending rather than expected spending based on joint probabilities.

Note that the risk-free rate rather than the asset return is justified for discounting spending needs. Although the cash flows themselves have risk, they have zero beta with the market and would, therefore, have no quantifiable market risk. In other words, there is no diversifiable risk associated with these cash flows.

Additionally, this estimate of core capital required does not include a safety reserve unless it was built into the annual spending estimate. Some estimates for safety reserve include up to two years of income to isolate investors from the psychological effects of fluctuations in invested capital and make it easier to follow the agreed strategy.

Example 2-1

David and Kenya Gosling have a probability of 68% and 69%, respectively, of being alive year 5 of their financial plan, when their annual spending need will be $274,000. The risk-free rate used by their advisor is 3%. The present value of their expected spending will be closest to:

    A. 212,908

    B. 236,354

    C. 246,819

Solution:

    A. First, determine the joint probability at least one will be alive:

$$p(\text{Survival}_{t,C_1C_2}) = p(C_1) + p(C_2) - p(C_1)p(C_2)$$

$$= 0.68 + 0.69 - (0.68)(0.69)$$

$$= 0.9008$$

Next, calculate the present value of the expected spending:

$$\text{Liability}_0 = \frac{0.9008 \times 274,000}{(1+0.03)^5} = 212,908.41$$

Monte Carlo Analysis

Monte Carlo analysis describes the estimation approach by which thousands of trials are completed to provide a range of potential outcomes for client assets. This approach estimates the asset base required to meet the clients' inflation-adjusted spending needs. Different market scenarios and client emergency needs can be programmed to affect the model and produce ending asset values.

After repeating the process thousands of times, the analyst can better understand the range of outcomes and, thus, the potential risk of the portfolio. The analyst can determine the core capital requirement that will meet the clients' spending requirement 95% of the time (95% confidence level). A higher confidence interval requires a greater core capital requirement.

Monte Carlo analysis differs from the mortality table method in that the returns are derived from parameters from assets recommended by the clients' strategic asset allocation or their actual portfolio of assets rather than the risk-free rate.

Monte Carlo analysis will typically allow various input sensitivities, such as market volatility, which increases standard deviation of portfolio returns and decreases expected returns. Lower portfolio returns, of course, decrease sustainability of the core capital or, alternately, increase the core capital requirement. Periodic withdrawals also decrease sustainability because they impact the portfolio's ability to recover. For example, when withdrawals are made during a period of low portfolio value, the portfolio value increases must be greater to adequately recover.

LESSON 3: TRANSFERRING EXCESS CAPITAL

LOS 12d: Evaluate the relative after-tax value of lifetime gifts and testamentary bequests. Vol 2, pp 288–299

LOS 12e: Explain the estate planning benefit of making lifetime gifts when gift taxes are paid by the donor, rather than the recipient. Vol 2, pp 288–299

LOS 12f: Evaluate the after-tax benefits of basic estate planning strategies, including generation skipping, spousal exemptions, valuation discounts, and charitable gifts. Vol 2, pp 288–299

EXCESS CAPITAL

Excess capital is the amount of capital greater than core capital. The plan for excess capital should allow the client to tax-efficiently transfer wealth according to their goals (e.g., philanthropic, inter-generational, etc.) and with the desired control or flexibility. Country specific tax and legal structures will likely affect the timing of excess capital transfers.

Lifetime Gifts and Testamentary Bequests

Jurisdictions that impose wealth transfer taxes on testamentary bequests (i.e., estate taxes) will find their citizens trying to avoid those taxes by gifting the money before they die. Jurisdictions wishing to avoid that loophole then impose gift taxes so that donors cannot avoid taxes on the annual gifts made in lieu of a later bequest.

Tax-free Gifts

Many countries allow taxpayers to give tax-free gifts during their lifetimes. In some cases, the amounts may be substantial. Other countries allow annual giving of a more modest amount, such as the U.S., which currently allows a tax-free gift of $14,000 annually. Over time, this reduces the taxpayer's taxable estate and increases the benefit of a gift via compounding. Whether the donor or the recipient pays the estate tax, however, determines just how much the compounding benefits the recipient.

The value of a tax-free gift made during the donor's lifetime relative to a bequest made via the estate is:

$$RV_{TFG} = \frac{FV_R}{FV_D} = \frac{\left[1 + r_R(1 - t_{I,R})\right]^n}{\left[1 + r_D(1 - t_{I,D})\right]^n (1 - t_{E,D})}$$

Where t_I and t_E are the tax on investment returns and estate, respectively, and subscripts D and R refer to the donor and recipient, respectively. The time period reflected by n in the numerator represents the expected time until the donor's death that the asset would transfer had it not been gifted. Therefore, the numerator shows the future after-tax value of the annual gift while the denominator shows the future after-tax value applicable to the same annual contribution, but transferred via bequest from the estate. If after-tax investment returns and the pre-tax returns associated with the gift are the same for the donor and recipient, then the formula reduces to $1 / (1 - t_{E,D})$.

Note that $RV - 1$ equals the percentage advantage (or disadvantage) of the numerator relative to the denominator.

Gifts Taxable to Recipient

Where the recipient R pays a tax on the gift at a rate of t_G, the formula becomes:

$$RV_{TG,R} = \frac{FV_R}{FV_D} = \frac{\left[1 + r_R(1 - t_{I,R})\right]^n (1 - t_{G,R})}{\left[1 + r_D(1 - t_{I,D})\right]^n (1 - t_{E,D})}$$

There may still be a benefit to the annual gifting program if the gift tax rate paid by the recipient is lower than the estate tax paid by the donor. If after-tax investment returns are the same for the recipient and the donor, then the formula reduces to $(1 - t_{G,R})/(1 - t_{E,D})$.

Where a *progressive rate schedule* for transfers applies, however, a tax savings will be possible by gifting amounts that fall into a lower rate tier of the schedule rather than the donor accumulating the earnings for tax at a higher rate tier of the schedule when the transfer is a bequest via the estate. Some countries, such as the U.S., have eliminated this benefit by combining a cumulative lifetime gift reduction to the amount excluded from a donor's taxable estate.

One common strategy is to gift higher-return assets while keeping lower-return assets in the estate. Higher return assets tend to have greater volatility, however, and there is no guarantee this strategy will result in the same terminal value as a strategy that gifted the assets in the donor's allocation. Failing to adjust gifting of assets that generate higher tax returns will also tend to change the portfolio allocation. Long-term after-tax asset allocation becomes more difficult in jurisdictions with frequent tax law changes, and the costs may outweigh the benefits.

Example 3-1

Smith lives in Country X, where he will pay a gift tax at his marginal 29% rate on any money gifted to him by his Uncle Jones, who lives in Country Y. Jones will be subject to a 40 percent tax on amounts remaining in his estate but during his life can make annual gifts of $15,000 to Smith without incurring estate tax. Smith will earn a return on his investments of 7% subject to a tax rate on investments of 20%. Jones can earn 9% on his investments, but will be subject to a tax rate on investments of 18%. If Jones' time horizon is 20 years, he should make:

A. annual gifts to Smith but not make a bequest from his estate.

B. a bequest from his estate but not make annual gifts to Smith.

C. either annual gifts to Smith or a bequest from his estate; the result is the same.

Solution:

B. The relative valuation is less than 1, so Jones should keep the money and give it as a bequest from his estate.

$$RV_{TG,R} = \frac{FV_R}{FV_D} = \frac{\left[1+r_R(1-t_{I,R})\right]^n(1-t_{G,R})}{\left[1+r_D(1-t_{I,D})\right]^n(1-t_{E,D})}$$

$$= \frac{\left[1+0.07(1-0.20)^{20}(1-0.29)\right]}{\left[1+0.09(1-0.18)^{20}(1-0.40)\right]}$$

$$= 0.847$$

Gifts Taxable to Donor

The prior discussion focused on gifts where tax was paid by the recipient. The economic value of the gift can increase where the donor, rather than the recipient, pays the gift taxes. This results because the gift tax paid by a donor reduces the size of the estate and the ultimate estate tax (which is usually quite high relative to tax rates on investment income). Where maximizing the wealth transfer amount, having the donor pay the tax also increases the recipient's net benefit for each lifetime transfer.

The relative value equation of a taxable gift when the donor pays the tax (and assuming the recipient's estate is not taxed as a result) then becomes:

$$RV_{TG,D} = \frac{FV_R}{FV_D} = \frac{\left[1+r_R(1-t_{I,R})\right]^n(1-t_{G,D}+(t_{G,D}t_{E,D}\times g/e)}{\left[1+r_D(1-t_{I,D})\right]^n(1-t_{E,D})}$$

The tax benefit from reducing the taxable estate (i.e., by the donor paying the gift tax) amounts to a *partial* gift tax credit with rate equal to $t_{G,R}\,t_{E,D}$. The size of the effective gift tax credit, then, equals the size of the gift multiplied by $t_{G,R}\,t_{E,D}$ multiplied by the gift as a percentage of the total estate.

Generation Skipping Transfers

HNW clients may attempt to pass excess assets down to their children's children (i.e., their grandchildren) using various methods known as *generation skipping transfers* (GSTs). For example, one approach is to avoid the second layer of gift or estate taxation (i.e., from children to grandchildren) by gifting enough to fund the children's lifestyle *and* the taxes from passing an inheritance to the grandchildren.

The client may wish, however, to gift money directly to the grandchildren, thus skipping the second intergenerational tax. The U.S. and possibly other jurisdictions have imposed a GST tax that prevents the client or the client's children from completely avoiding the second tax that would have been incurred as assets were passed from the client's children to their grandchildren.

Spousal Exemptions

Gratuitous transfer tax exclusion may apply to smaller estates in which each spouse may give some level of gifts free of estate or gift tax. The estate and gift tax exclusion may be *unified*, as in the U.S., such that notional tax on gifts during a decedent's lifetime reduces the exclusion from the estate tax at death. This addresses the problem of wealthy individuals gifting too much during life in order to avoid estate tax at death.

Jurisdictions typically allow one spouse to transfer unlimited wealth—either in the form of gifts during life or at death—to another spouse without any tax consequence. In these cases, it may make sense for the first decedent spouse to transfer the exclusion amount to someone other than the second spouse. For example, a couple with a $1 million estate at the death of the first spouse could have given some portion of the decedent spouse's half and avoided the tax on it at the second spouse's death. In some cases, an exclusion amount for a married couple may be used by both spouses, reduced for that portion used by the first decedent spouse.

Valuation Discounts

Levying tax against transfer of exchange traded securities is not difficult because values are easily obtained. In the case of closely held companies, valuation will likely require the input of professionals at valuing such assets. Such professionals often choose a higher cost of capital to perform the valuation or otherwise discount valuation in order to recognize additional risks (i.e., lack of liquidity).

If the married couple controls the company, it may be possible to gift portions of it in some way that eliminates the control premium of the pre-distribution shares in the company. Discounts for lack of control are not additive with illiquidity discounts, however, and may be part of the reason the shares may be somewhat illiquid. For example, a lack of liquidity discount of 10 percent and lack of control discount of 25 percent may result in a total discount closer to 25 percent than 35 percent.

Both lack of liquidity and lack of control can be accomplished by placing the assets to be gifted into a *family limited partnership* (FLP). FLPs may even be constructed using cash and marketable securities rather than closely held business interests, but will generally be allowed less discount for transfer tax purposes. In addition to satisfying the family dynamics of more equitable distribution of gains and losses, FLPs can help the heirs gain access to hedge funds and other asset management situations requiring high minimum investment amounts.

Deemed Dispositions

Some countries treat transfer of appreciated assets as if the decedent had disposed of them. Such *deemed dispositions* are then taxed on unrealized capital gains rather than the entire value of the asset. For assets likely to continue appreciating, it may make sense to transfer the asset prior to the decedent's death in order to extend the capital gain without extension. The strategy makes even better sense in jurisdictions without tax on inter vivos gifts.

ESTATE PLANNING IN A GLOBAL CONTEXT

Charitable Gratuitous Transfers

While gratuitous transfers to charities (and sometimes political organizations) are seldom subject to gift tax, many jurisdictions provide income tax deductions to eleemosynary institutions. Charities are frequently also exempt from income tax on earnings on investments. The value of a charitable gift relative to a bequest from a grantor can be quantified as:

$$RV_{CG} = \frac{FV_R}{FV_D} = \frac{(1+r_R)^n + t_{OI,D}\left[1+r_D(1-t_{I,D})\right]^n(1-t_{E,D})}{\left[1+r_D(1-t_{I,D})\right]^n(1-t_{E,D})}$$

The second term in the numerator recognizes the benefit of a tax deduction from the donor's taxable ordinary income (OI). This allows the donor to either increase the potential donation to a charity or to reduce the cost of a given amount of donation.

The relative value of a charitable gift will generally have high relative value because it:

- Provides a tax deduction against ordinary income;
- Escapes gift tax;
- Escapes estate tax; and
- Accumulates tax free within the charity.

Example 3-2

A country with 60% estate tax does not charge tax on qualifying charitable donations. Donors also receive a tax deduction against ordinary income for the charitable donation. High net worth investors may be subject to ordinary income tax at a 39% rate. Investment income is subject to a 20% tax rate. The gifted amount will earn a return for the donor or the recipient of 7%. The value of the charitable contribution relative to a bequest over a 20-year horizon will be *closest* to:

A. 3.2

B. 3.6

C. 4.2

Solution:

B. The relative value to the donor of the charitable gift is:

$$RV_{CG} = \frac{FV_R}{FV_D} = \frac{(1+r_R) + t_{OI,D}\left[1+r_D(1+t_{I,D})\right]^n(1-t_{E,D})}{\left[1+r_D(1-t_{I,D})\right]^n(1-t_{E,D})}$$

$$= \frac{(1+0.07)^{20} + 0.39\left[1+0.07(1-0.20)\right]^{20}(1-060)}{\left[1+0.07(1-0.20)\right]^{20}(1-0.60)}$$

$$= 3.64$$

LESSON 4: ESTATE PLANNING TOOLS

LOS 12g: Explain the basic structure of a trust and discuss the differences between revocable and irrevocable trusts. Vol 2, pp 299–301

ESTATE PLANNING STRUCTURES

While various strategies allow donors to optimize their tax liabilities against the backdrop of accomplishing gifting goals, various other structures are also available to manipulate the timing or control of various assets. One of those structures, Family Limited Partnerships, has already been described in conjunction with limiting tax liability by decreasing valuation of gifted assets.

Trusts

A *trust* is a structure in which a *trustee* holds and manages assets donated by the *grantor* (or *settlor*) for the benefit of the *beneficiaries*. Trusts often offer grantors the ability to transfer assets without the publicity associated with a probated bequest. There are two general trust dimensions:

1. *Irrevocable or revocable*—An *irrevocable trust* cannot be changed by the grantor, and the trustee files tax-related documents and pays relevant tax from trust assets. A *revocable trust* may be dissolved by the grantor and the assets returned, but the grantor, rather than the trustee, will be responsible for filing tax-related documents and paying relevant tax from the assets. Irrevocable trusts typically provide better protection from legal claims against the grantor.
2. *Fixed or discretionary*—*Fixed trusts* distribute assets to beneficiaries according to a fixed schedule or formula, often including the earliest time at which the assets are to be distributed (i.e., at the beneficiary's 21st birthday). *Discretionary trusts* allow the trustee to distribute assets for the general welfare of the beneficiary at the trustee's discretion. The beneficiaries' creditors cannot typically attach discretionary trust assets to satisfy debts. Fixed trusts will typically be used to make payments at specific times for specific purposes, often to avoid a spendthrift beneficiary from depleting the trust.

A possible motivation for a discretionary trust might be to prevent an antagonist spouse from gaining control of trust assets in a divorce settlement. Gifts and trusts may also be used to circumvent forced heirship rules.

In many countries, income is taxed according to a progressive schedule. By disaggregating the donor's income into several trusts, the tax liability may be reduced. An irrevocable discretionary trust may allow the trustee to structure trust distributions to consider the beneficiary's tax situation, distributing less during periods when the beneficiary has higher ordinary earned income. Each situation on the actual exam differs according to the relative benefits of the tax on income, estate, etc.

In some countries, assets can be transferred from a donor to a recipient in a way that avoids estate taxes on a bequest while reducing the donor's taxable estate by the amount of taxes paid on the trust.

Foundations

Donors in some jurisdictions may elect to establish foundations for a certain purpose (e.g., education, philanthropy, etc.). A foundation, like a trust, survives the donor and can require funds to be used for purposes established by the donor. Foundations, unlike trusts, are based on civil law and are considered separate persons. Therefore, the donor's nationality or residence may determine the choice of trust or foundation.

LOS 12h: Explain how life insurance can be a tax-efficient means of wealth transfer. Vol 2, pp 302–303

Life Insurance

Life insurance allows the donor to transfer assets (in the form of a *premium*) to an insurer who then promises to make a payment to a trust or individuals at the donor's death without the expense and time delay of probate. It becomes quite useful in situations where a jurisdiction does not recognize trusts (e.g., civil law countries in Europe and South America) or is suspicious of them.

Many jurisdictions allow transfer of death benefits to avoid taxation and reporting. Premiums are not subject to gratuitous transfer taxes and yet help reduce the donor's estate without being subject to estate taxes. Further, many jurisdictions allow assets within the life insurance structure to accumulate tax free. Although withdrawals of cash value by the donor may be subject to income tax, these can be avoided by taking a loan against the policy rather than receiving the cash value outright.

To avoid abuses of the tax benefits associated with life insurance, many jurisdictions require a certain level of risk inherent in the insured and that the policy owner must have an actual interest in the insured (e.g., you cannot insure the life of Bill Gates, unless you have an actual insurable interest).

Life insurance may also be used as a liquidity enhancement technique to pay inheritance taxes for beneficiaries at the insured's death. This becomes especially important when transfer of illiquid assets creates a liability to the beneficiary who has limited funds to pay the tax on them.

Also, proceeds from a life insurance policy may help an owner avoid forced heirship rules. Premiums and cash value in the policy cannot usually be attached by creditors. Insurance may be used to fund a discretionary trust when the ultimate beneficiary is unable or unwilling to manage their own finances.

Controlled Foreign Corporation

A *controlled foreign corporation* (CFC) is a company located in a tax jurisdiction different from the controlling taxpayer's home jurisdiction. CFCs will typically be established in jurisdictions with low or no corporate income tax, and dividends will be taxed, often at a favorable rate, when distributed from the corporation.

CFC rules may be triggered at ownership percentages specific to the taxpayer's home jurisdiction, but often over 50% ownership, which tax shareholders on a *deemed distribution* of corporate earnings even if dividends are not paid.

LESSON 5: CROSS-BORDER ESTATE PLANNING

LOS 12i: Discuss the two principal systems (source jurisdiction and residence jurisdiction) for establishing a country's tax jurisdiction. Vol 2, pp 303–306

LOS 12j: Discuss the possible income and estate tax consequences of foreign situated assets and foreign-sourced income. Vol 2, pp 303–306

ESTATE PLANNING ACROSS BORDERS

Assets located outside the owner's home country may generate income subject to taxation in both the country where the assets are located as well as by the owner's home country. In addition, estate taxes may be levied in each country. Even passing assets located in the owner's home country to beneficiaries outside the owner's home country may generate double taxation.

The Hague Conference and Convention

In order to simplify and standardize cross-border legal processes, The *Hague Conference on International Private Law* developed various conventions that member countries agree to become party to recognition. Parties to the Hague Conference may agree to allow non-member companies to participate if they agree to be bound by a treaty.

While 39 countries have agreed to the form of a will used internationally, the U.S. has not agreed. Separate wills may be required for different jurisdictions, especially where real estate is involved.

The *Hague Convention of the Law Applicable to Trusts and on Their Recognition* provides convergence on the regulation of trust relationships. Only 12 countries participated in this convention, largely owing to non-recognition of trusts in Europe and Latin America.

Source and Residence Jurisdiction

Most countries use a *residence jurisdiction* system in which income from all countries is taxed to the person who claims residence within a country's borders. A country's citizens who do not claim residence within its borders are not subject to tax on their income from that country. A few countries use a *source jurisdiction* that taxes income earned within its borders.

Tax authorities use varying methods to determine residency:

- *Objective standards*—Number of days of physical presence within the borders.
- *Subjective standards*—Degree of economic and family ties to the country (e.g., owning a business or residence, family members living within the country, etc.).

The U.S. taxes citizens and non-citizen residents on their income regardless of where sourced, as well as on testamentary transfers. In contrast, the U.K. does not tax *resident, non-domiciled* (RND) persons within its borders. This makes the U.K. particularly attractive for high net worth (HNW) individuals who can locate assets outside the U.K. but wish to reside or do business there for at least some portion of the year.

Remember, you do not need to know the specific tax rules of any particular country. Just be aware of these terms if they are used on the exam.

The residence principle, should it apply, would levy estate taxes on assets worldwide, with some jurisdictions excluding real estate located in other jurisdictions. The source principle, however, would tax assets within a particular country or transferred into that country. The U.S. taxes all assets on citizens and residents regardless of residence or source. Foreign estate tax credits and exclusions help mitigate double taxation that would inevitably result from such a system.

Exit tax may be payable on unrealized capital gains for individuals transferring assets outside the jurisdiction as the result of giving up residency or citizenship (i.e., *deemed disposition*). Such a tax is generally not applicable to assets transferred among E.U. countries, but would apply if the assets are transferred outside the E.U. Income earned over a "shadow period" after expatriation may also be taxable.

LOS 12k: Evaluate a client's tax liability under each of three basic methods (credit, exemption, and deduction) that a country may use to provide relief from double taxation. Vol 2, pp 303–306

Double Taxation

Several types of conflict can occur between countries with regard to creating a tax liability:

- *Residence-residence conflict*—Countries dispute the residence of the taxpayer.
- *Source-source conflict*—Countries dispute the source of the taxable item, such as when assets in one country are managed from another country.
- *Residence-source conflict*—Where a non-citizen is a resident of a residence jurisdiction country but is a citizen of a source jurisdiction country. In this case, residence countries are usually required to provide relief, if any, from double taxation with the source of the income becoming the primary jurisdiction.

Tax Code Relief

In the *credit method*, the residence jurisdiction reduces taxes payable in its jurisdiction by the amount of tax paid in source jurisdiction countries. The allowable tax credit cannot exceed tax payable within the residence jurisdiction country. For example, if the taxpayer must pay a $500 tax liability in the residence jurisdiction country, but has $400 liability due from a source jurisdiction country, the taxpayer will pay $400 to the source jurisdiction country and $100 to the residence jurisdiction country.

$$t_{CM} = Max(t_{RC}, t_{SC})$$

In the *exemption method*, the source jurisdiction income is excluded from taxable income in the residence jurisdiction. Continuing the previous example, the taxpayer would have only the $400 liability to the source country jurisdiction and $0 liability to the residence jurisdiction country. Only a few countries have adopted this method.

$$t_{EM} = t_{SC}$$

In the *deduction method*, the residence jurisdiction country allows a deduction from taxable income for taxes paid to the source country. Clearly, this will result in a higher tax liability than either the credit or the exemption method. The tax rate payable under the deduction method can be described as:

$$t_{DM} = t_{RC} + t_{SC} - t_{RC}t_{SC}$$

Example 5-1

A citizen-resident of Country X, a residence-based jurisdiction, is subject to estate taxes on foreign property at a 60% rate in Country X and 40% in Country Y, a source-based jurisdiction. Countries X and Y have a double taxation treaty specifying the deduction method of resolving residence-source conflicts. This taxpayer will have an effective rate on the testamentary asset transfer closest to:

A. 20%

B. 40%

C. 80%

Solution:

C. The deduction method tax rate is:

$$t_{DM} = t_{RC} + t_{SC} - t_{RC}t_{SC}$$
$$= 0.40 + 0.60 - 0.40(0.60)$$
$$= 76\%$$

Treaty Relief

Double taxation treaties (DTTs) promote increased capital mobility and facilitate trade by resolving residence-source conflicts between countries. Nearly all treaties follow the OECD model treaty format, which specifies dividend and investment income should be taxed in the jurisdiction paying the income and recommends the source country withhold at a 15 percent rate for dividends and 10 percent for interest income. Capital gains are then taxed in the residence jurisdiction except for immovable property, the gain on which is taxed in the source country.

DTTs do not resolve source-source conflict, but may resolve residence-residence conflicts based on criteria such as:

- Location of primary residence;
- Center of vital interests;
- Habitual dwelling; and
- Citizenship.

LOS 12l: Discuss how increasing international transparency and information exchange among tax authorities affect international estate planning. Vol 2, pp 310–311

Transparency

Financial advisors may engage in minimizing tax liability (*tax avoidance*) but should not engage in circumventing tax liability through misrepresentation or failing to report relevant information (*tax evasion*). Banks in countries with secrecy laws can provide an important benefit to HNWIs in terms of politics, privacy, efficiency, security, and family dynamics but should not be used to shield otherwise taxable income from view of taxing authorities.

Most banks in countries with privacy laws have become *qualified intermediaries* (QIs), which requires them to report asset transactions on U.S. citizens but not on non-U.S. citizens. The reporting will only occur at the request of the U.S. authorities. The European Union Savings Directive (EUSD) collects taxes made in a source country for the benefit of the taxpayer's residence country. Austria, Belgium, and Luxembourg, however, do not participate, preferring instead to levy a tax against the earnings at the source and transfer the pooled tax revenues to the residence country. Authorities now frequently accumulate credit card transaction information on non-citizens and forward it to their home countries.

In short, wealth management strategies should be based on firm economic and tax-related benefits rather than attempting to hide transactions behind archaic bank secrecy laws that will likely soon become irrelevant.

STUDY SESSION 6:
PRIVATE WEALTH MANAGEMENT (2)

READING 13: CONCENTRATED SINGLE-ASSET POSITIONS

Time to complete: 1.5 to 2 hours

Reading Summary: High net worth clients often have concentrated positions in assets that served to create their wealth, usually in the form of publicly-traded stock, a privately-held company, or real estate investments. HNWs may ultimately need to sell or otherwise *monetize* (i.e., unlock the monetary value without selling) these highly concentrated positions to provide funds or better manage risk.

Investment advisors can play a key role in helping clients understand various options for reallocating capital out of concentrated positions to better meet their long-term goals and objectives.

This lesson will provide you with the tools to:

1. Recognize and explain risks associated with concentrated positions in a single asset;
2. Describe how asset managers implement goal-based planning in managing concentrated positions; and
3. Understand and discuss the financial and psychological considerations in managing and reallocating concentrated positions.

LESSON 1: CONCENTRATED SINGLE-ASSET POSITIONS: OVERVIEW AND INVESTMENT RISKS

LOS 13a: Explain investment risks associated with a concentrated position in a single asset and discuss the appropriateness of reducing such risks. Vol 2, pp 322–327

GENERAL CONSIDERATIONS

A concentrated position has no universally agreed definition, although some practitioners have suggested it must be at least 25% of the client's net worth to be considered as such. Part of the confusion is that a particular position may be less than 25% of the client's total net worth, but represents a significant percentage of an asset class (e.g., a stock that comprises a high percentage of the total securities portfolio). This latter type of concentration must also be managed.

Such positions were often acquired many years ago or over time, and may have appreciated significantly since original purchase. There may be tax implications to disposition of the asset.

Concentrated positions often face both systematic and non-systematic risk, with inadequate risk-adjusted returns. For example, advisors should consider opportunity costs of holding underperforming company stock or large tracts of land that produce no income.

Investment Risks

Systematic risk describes the portion of risk attributable to the market or market segment as a whole. It cannot be avoided or diversified. While the capital asset pricing model (CAPM) addresses the asset's variability relative to financial markets, other models capture broader aspects, such as changes in business activity levels, unexpected inflation, and parts of equity market risk unexplained by macroeconomic factors. When human capital correlates with such market risk, unexpected job loss may occur at the very time it will be most difficult to cash out an equity portfolio.

Non-systematic risk represents the portion of risk that, at least to some extent, may be diversified. It is the risk specific to a particular asset that will not necessarily apply to all assets within the same class. This is known as *company risk* when related to publicly-held stock or ownership of a privately-held business. A concentrated position diminishes benefits available from portfolio diversification, and a negative event that applies to that concentrated position can result in significant and sometimes irreparable damage to an investor's portfolio.

Property risk describes the non-systematic risk specific to a particular asset. For example, an event could trigger devaluation for a particular property that would not be applicable to similar properties within the same market or the real estate market in general. Examples of this might be finding contamination on land associated with a property. Something as simple as vacancy could be described as a property-specific risk if the vacating tenants would require a great deal of time to replace.

LESSON 2: GENERAL PRINCIPLES OF MANAGING CONCENTRATED SINGLE-ASSET POSITIONS

LOS 13b: Describe typical objectives in managing concentrated positions. Vol 2, pp 327–328

General Management Principles

This section looks at general principles for managing concentrated positions.

Objectives

Financial advisors often look at the following objectives when managing the client's concentrated position:

- *Risk reduction*—The financial advisor should dimension the risks from the position, the risks of changing the position (i.e., loss of operational control of a closely held business), and the potential rewards from making the change.
- *Cash flow optimization*—Illiquid positions often need to be sold or monetized in order to meet a client's spending objectives, legacy fulfillment desires, and charitable inclinations.
- *Tax efficiency*—Structuring transactions to avoid or defer a taxable event, or to minimize the overall impact of taxes in conjunction with the client's stated objectives.

LOS 13c: Discuss tax consequences and illiquidity as considerations affecting the management of concentrated positions in publicly traded common shares, privately held businesses, and real estate. Vol 2, pp 328–331

LOS 13d: Discuss capital market and institutional constraints on an investor's ability to reduce a concentrated position. Vol 2, pp 328–331

General Constraints

It may not always be necessary or desirable for a client to eliminate a concentrated position. For example, concentrated stock positions may be desirable or necessary to maintain if:

- An executive received shares with the expectation or requirement that the shares be maintained, in order that the company could tie the executive's fortunes with the company's fortunes.
- The share owner wishes to maintain a control position in the company.
- The share owner wishes to maintain the long-term appreciation potential of the shares but needs to monetize a current income stream.

Ownership interests in a privately-held company may be desirable or necessary to maintain if:

- Significant capital has been invested but could not yet be monetized (e.g., as in a startup).
- The owner wishes to maintain total control.
- The owner wishes to confer part of his position to executive management over time.
- The position is part of an inter-generational transfer objective.

Ownership interests in real estate may be desirable or necessary to maintain if:

- The asset is essential to the operation of other business assets in the investor's portfolio.
- The asset was purchased with the idea of significant price appreciation over time.
- The asset is part of an inter-generational transfer objective.

Institutional Constraints

Choice of a strategy for selling or monetizing concentrated positions depends on governing law, the availability of finance, and other institutional constraints.

Margin Lending Rules

Margin describes the percentage of equity that must be maintained in an account and, thus, how much borrowing may occur against the pledged assets. Under a *rules-based* system, the use of margin is constrained by rules. In the U.S., for example, margin of 50 percent will be required for a *purpose loan* to purchase equity securities, even if the securities are fully hedged by a put. A *risk-based* system, by contrast, will allow the holder of the hedged securities to margin a much greater percentage, perhaps even up to 100 percent, depending on the risk to the portfolio. The loan against the entire portfolio is also allowed in the U.S. if the purpose is not to purchase additional equity securities.

A *prepaid variable forward* (i.e., an instrument comprising both a collar—long put below and short call above the respective strike prices—and a loan) are not subject to the margin rules and become *off-balance-sheet debt*. For all practical purposes, the prepaid variable forward acts as a sale with the loan being the proceeds, but does not trigger the capital gains tax that would be applicable had an actual sale taken place.

Securities Laws and Regulations

Individuals cannot trade on material, non-public information that routinely becomes available to executives in a company. They must, however, comply with reporting requirements. The type, timing, or quantity of a sale may be subject to limitations.

Contractual Restrictions and Mandates

Contractual restrictions (e.g., initial public offering "lockups") and employer mandates (e.g., *blackout periods* when insiders must not sell their shares) greatly restrict how and when insiders sell shares. Privately-held companies may require a *right of first refusal* that limits an insider's ability to sell to an outside party without first offering the interest to current shareholders or owners at the same price and under the same conditions.

Capital Market Limitations

Dealers require the ability to manage their risk of being counterparties to transactions. Dealers may be reluctant to enter a transaction that could monetize a concentrated position if they are unable to source the proper liquidity to borrow or short the position. Many dealers will avoid such positions after an IPO when the trading patterns are still uncertain. Making the owner's shares available to the dealer potentially qualifies the shares as a sale subject to taxation, possibly undermining the tax deferral objectives of the strategy.

LOS 13e: Discuss psychological considerations that may make an investor reluctant to reduce his or her exposure to a concentrated position. Vol 2, pp 331–334

Behavioral Considerations

As with establishing any client relationship, an advisor should identify cognitive and emotional biases in their clients holding concentrated positions. These are considered rather exhaustively elsewhere, but are listed here for convenience.

Emotional Biases

An advisor may not be able to overcome an emotional bias but must instead work around it. Some examples are:

- Naive extrapolation of past returns
- Status quo bias (preference against change)
- Overconfidence and familiarity (illusion of knowledge)
- Endowment and loyalty (leading to an unwarranted premium)

Pointing out the bias will usually not be effective; after all, it's emotional. Asking the client to describe how they would invest a similar amount received in cash might circumvent the emotional nature of requiring them to first sell anything. The result from the desired strategy can then be compared against the "do nothing" strategy to uncover the benefits from making a change.

Cognitive Biases

Cognitive biases may be easier to overcome and may result from something as simple as an incorrect rule of thumb. Such biases include:

- Illusion of control
- Conservatism (reluctance to update beliefs)
- Confirmation (search for or observing only what confirms beliefs)
- Anchoring and adjustment (viewing decisions as adjustments to an initial position)
- Availability heuristic (using the ease of recalling events as probability of their occurrence)

Investors typically have less emotional investment in cognitive biases, and may correct these errors simply by having them called to attention.

Example 2-1

A former member of XYZ company's executive management team has a concentrated position in its stock. He believes that working for the company made him the man he is today and has severe reservations about selling his shares to diversify his portfolio. He also believes he can tell how well the company is doing even though he no longer has access to insider information. This client could *best* be described as suffering from:

A. endowment and status quo biases.

B. endowment and overconfidence biases.

C. availability heuristic and overconfidence bias.

Solution:

B. This client has endowment bias related to his belief the company "made him what he is today" and overconfidence bias because he believes he knows more about the inner workings of the firm than he actually does.

> We discuss cognitive and emotional biases in more detail in the Behavioral Finance section.

LOS 13f: Describe advisers' use of goal-based planning in managing concentrated positions. Vol 2, pp 334–337

Goal-Based Planning

Goal-based planning can highlight the dangers of maintaining a risky concentrated position in a portfolio. This works best by performing asset allocation in three "risk buckets":

1. *Personal risk bucket*—Forces the client to consider a dramatic decrease in lifestyle or even poverty. Therefore, there is little risk available in this bucket but the assets yield commensurately lower return.
2. *Market risk bucket*—Focuses on maintaining the client's current lifestyle. There is market risk and return.
3. *Aspirational risk bucket*—The goal for this bucket is to substantially increase wealth and standard of living. Clients then allocate their privately-owned businesses, concentrated stock positions, investment real estate, stock options, etc. to this bucket.

Personal risk and market risk buckets are usually referred to as *primary capital*, while assets in the aspirational bucket are called *surplus capital* (or *discretionary wealth*). By framing in terms of these buckets, clients with concentrated positions can often see without further prompting that they have too much allocated to the aspirational risk bucket, but not enough to the market risk and personal risk buckets.

In determining whether to sell or monetize the concentrated positions, it can help to understand how much will be required to fully fund the primary and surplus capital requirements:

Current value of liquid assets not in the concentrated position.
Less: PV of capital required to meet spending needs (primary capital)
Primary capital surplus / (gap)
Plus: Current value of concentrated position
Less: PV of capital required to meet aspirational goals (secondary capital)
Total capital surplus / (gap)

If a primary capital gap exists, financial advisors can easily point to the shortfall as a necessary reallocation from the concentrated position. A total capital surplus can help determine how much of the primary capital gap (if any) could be funded by selling or monetizing the concentrated position. Then, the advisor can help the client begin dealing with any emotional aspects related to the sale or monetization.

Example 2-2

Alvin Peabody has primary capital needs of $15 million and long-term aspirational goals with a present funding value of $25 million. He has $1.5 million of protective assets, $3 million of market assets, and $50 million in commercial real estate located in downtown Chicago that he owns free and clear. Which of the following is the *best* course of action with regard to possible reallocation of his concentrated position?

A. Do nothing.

B. Borrow against the commercial real estate to fund adequate primary capital.

C. Sell the investment property and invest the proceeds in a market-based financial asset.

Solution:

B. Peabody currently has primary capital requirements of $15 million, but only has primary capital of $4.5 million ($1.5mm + $3mm). He therefore has a primary capital shortfall of $10.5 million. This amount could easily be monetized from the investment real estate position leaving him with $39.5 million ($50mm – $10.5mm) in the investment real estate to fund his long-term aspirational goals. This could easily be accomplished with loans against the real estate. Selling the real estate could trigger the capital gains tax.

LOS 13g: Explain uses of asset location and wealth transfers in managing concentrated positions. Vol 2, pp 337–340

Asset Location Considerations

Asset location refers to the type of account holding funds; that is, whether it is taxable, tax-deferred, etc. The structure of an account can often override the tax treatment of earnings from the account. For example, dividends, interest, and capital gains may each be given special tax treatment in a taxable account, but the proceeds from a tax-deferred account may either be given favorable tax treatment or taxed at an ordinary income rate depending on the rules for the jurisdiction.

The asset allocation decision determines the risk-return tradeoffs necessary to satisfy investor preferences. The *asset location decision*—distinct from the asset allocation decision—specifies the structures that provide the optimal tax profile. Concentrated positions require a combination of the asset location decision and transfer strategies (i.e., gift or bequest) to minimize transfer taxes.

Prior to Appreciation

Advisors who can begin working with clients before appreciation has become too great a factor in the decision may be able to add value with simple strategies such as direct gifts to family members or estate freeze strategies (e.g., irrevocable trusts, family limited partnerships, etc.). Estate freeze strategies essentially transfer the future appreciation to the beneficiary of the strategy. While the gift may be accumulated against the transferor's gift and estate tax exemptions and exclusions, the appreciation is not.

In the case of a closely held corporation, donating the owner-controlled common shares to a trust would essentially put corporate decisions in the hands of a trust. To avoid this, owner-controlled common shares may be exchanged for voting preferred shares (with essentially 100% of the value) and non-voting common shares (with no value). The owner retains control because votes remain with the preferred shares and the common shares can be gifted more or less tax free to the heirs. At the owner's death, the preferred shares are passed (and taxed) at close to their original value because there will be minimal appreciation (if any) for shares that have a stated face amount and pay regular interest like a bond. If interest rates increase, the preferred share value may actually decline.

Example 2-3

Brenda Marburg, age 35, owns a candy company with a tax basis of $1 million and market value of $5 million. She wishes to retain control of the company during her lifetime, and continue receiving funds from the company. She hopes to avoid paying estate and gift tax on an appreciated value for the company when she dies in 40 years or so. Her *best* course of action to pass ownership of the company to her heirs with minimal tax consequences is to:

A. sell the business and establish a trust.

B. add debt to the capital structure, and use the proceeds to buy back all common shares.

C. exchange common shares for voting preferred and non-voting common shares, and then gift the common shares to heirs.

Solution:

C. Marburg can retain control of the company while essentially freezing the value of her gift at the market value of the preferred shares. At her death, the low basis value preferred shares will pass to the heirs with favorable tax consequences compared to passed fully appreciated voting common shares. Selling the business will result in an immediate gains tax on $4 million gain, and she will definitely lose control of the company now or in the future.

After Appreciation

A *family limited partnership* (FLP) may be an appropriate way to minimize transfer taxes for highly appreciated assets such as shares in a privately-held company. In this strategy, the donor's common shares are exchanged for shares in the general partnership, as well as limited partner shares. Some or all of the limited partner shares may be transferred at a low basis (and low tax liability) because they lack marketability, liquidity, and control. The share donors retain control through the general partnership.

LESSON 3: MANAGING THE RISK OF CONCENTRATED SINGLE-STOCK POSITIONS

LOS 13h: Describe strategies for managing concentrated positions in publicly traded common shares. Vol 2, pp 340–356

LOS 13i: Discuss tax considerations in the choice of hedging strategy. Vol 2, pp 340–356

LOS 13l: Evaluate and recommend techniques for tax efficiently managing the risks of concentrated positions in publicly traded common stock, privately held businesses, and real estate. Vol 2, pp 340–356

Single-Stock Concentration

Dealing with concentrated equity positions usually revolves around selling, monetizing, or preserving value.

Tax Considerations

Although tax regimes may address all the ways to dispose of securities, the laws are not always internally consistent as to tax liability. This presents opportunities to minimize tax liability by selecting an appropriate strategy. This primarily occurs because financial professionals innovate and tax authorities respond afterward, often using inconsistent treatment for the same economic objective.

Non-Tax Considerations

Various methods of minimizing taxes have consequences outside the actual statutory tax rate, such as:

- *Minimum size constraints*—OTC derivatives generally have a minimum size of $3 million, while exchange-traded derivatives have a smaller minimum.
- *Flexibility of terms*—OTC derivatives allow the investor to tailor terms within various parameters, while exchange-traded derivatives are standardized.
- *Counterparty risk*—OTC derivatives typically have counterparty risk that varies with the financial strength of the counterparty. Exchange-traded derivatives have a clearinghouse with significant financial resources as intermediary to the transaction, standing ready to pay if a counterparty fails to honor a commitment. In addition, exchange-traded derivatives have daily mark-to-market, which limits counterparty risk to one day's gain. This is negotiable in OTC derivatives.

- *Early termination*—OTC derivatives require renegotiation to close out the contract prior to maturity. Equity-traded derivate positions can be closed out by an offsetting transaction.
- *Fee transparency*—Fees for OTC derivatives will often be embedded in the transaction price. All fees must be identified on exchange-traded derivative transactions.
- *Price discovery*—Prices are negotiated on OTC derivatives, and are often obscured due to fees that are embedded in the transactions price. Prices for exchange-traded instruments are established in open markets, where buyers and sellers can quickly adjust prices.

Strategies

Owners of a concentrated equity position will tend to employ a strategy that best meets their needs and minimizes tax liability.

Monetization

Monetization generally means that the cash value of the asset is realized with a strategy other than outright sale. In addition to avoiding any tax due upon sale, monetization may:

- Allow the owner to retain control;
- Avoid securities law restrictions against equity sales; and
- Avoid contractual restrictions (e.g., IPO lockup, employment agreements, etc.) against equity sales.

The first step in monetization strategy is to remove the risk. However, hedging strategies require careful attention to applicable taxes and invite scrutiny from the tax authorities. In many cases, removing the risk allows the owner to obtain a high loan-to-value (LTV) debt position against the securities. Loan proceeds may then be invested in a diversified portfolio of securities.

Removing the stock market risk may take several forms:

- *Short sale against the box*—Because the owner already has the shares in an account (i.e., the box), shorting the shares offsets any economic impact to the long position. This essentially transfers the shares into a money market position and the owner will earn that rate of return, which can often offset costs of the short sale (e.g., fees and margin interest). This may not be available in the U.S. or other jurisdictions if it were to be considered a *constructive sale* (i.e., has the economic effect of actually selling the shares).
- *Total return equity swap*—An owner of a concentrated position might exchange appreciation and earnings on the low-basis equity shares for loss of value in the shares plus LIBOR plus a dealer spread. This fully hedges the underlying equity position and pays the owner a money market rate. This will typically have slightly higher expenses than a short against the box.
- *Forward conversion with options*—This strategy involves buying long puts and selling calls against the underlying security. Both the long puts and short calls have the same strike price. If the price increases, calls would be exercised and the owner would deliver the shares. If the price decreases, the owner could exercise puts and receive the proceeds. This essentially locks in the price to the owner no matter

which way the price moves. This is also an essentially riskless position that should pay the money market return and allow a high loan-to-value.

- *Equity forward contract*—The owner enters a contract to deliver the underlying shares, and the buyer agrees to pay a certain price for the shares. The forward price recognizes a money market rate of return to the share owner. Because the position is riskless, the transaction can be undertaken at a high loan-to-value.

In any case, typical monetization strategies share these characteristics:

- Create a riskless position;
- Allow very high loan-to-value debt positions; and
- Lower borrowing costs with the money market return.

Taxes have historically been tied to realization of a capital gain on the asset itself, thus allowing most monetization strategies to escape taxation on the underlying long asset. However, tax may still be payable on either the long or short position if it is realized. Other considerations depend on the tax regime:

- Short-term losses are generally preferable to long-term;
- Current deductibility of losses is generally preferred to adding the loss to the cost basis of the underlying;
- Current deductibility of carrying costs is generally preferred to adding the loss to the cost basis of the underlying; and
- Preferably, the hedge will have no impact on taxation of dividends or other distributions from the underlying.

Hedging

In this reading, hedging refers to a situation where the client wishes to protect against the downside but also retain some upside appreciation. Hedging may be useful where the owner wishes to retain a control position within the underlying and protect against losses but wishes to participate in additional gains:

- *Puts*—Buying a put locks in the floor price while allowing continued appreciation, and defers any gains tax until the underlying is sold. Premiums for out-of-the-money puts can be expensive, so owners will typically purchase out-of-the-money puts (i.e., self-insures down to the strike price), puts with shorter maturity, or use a *put spread* (i.e., buy the higher price puts and sell lower price puts). Less expensive knock-out puts that expire early if the put price is reached can be obtained from OTC dealers, subject to a high minimum size requirement.
- *Cashless collars*—The owner purchases puts as above, but sells out-of-the-money calls with the same maturity and premium. These are sometimes referred to as *zero-premium collars*, although there are actually offsetting premiums paid and received. There is no cash out of the owner's pocket, and the use of a spread order lowers the margin requirement although there are two simultaneously executed contracts. Some investors wishing to participate more on the upside may increase the call price (and lower their premium received) while decreasing the put price (and lower their premium paid), or pay part of a higher put price out of pocket. Combinations of a put spread and call can be sold, which allows a higher price call (with lower premium income) to be offset by selling a put. The owner will be exposed to losses below the strike price of the short put.

In both strategies, the owner retains all rights to distributions associated with the equity securities, control over voting rights, participates in upside potential, and avoids gains tax on a sale of the underlying. The owner may then use a margin loan to monetize the position.

Alternatively, a *prepaid variable forward* combines a collar and borrowing in the same instrument. The *variable* comes into play because the number of shares to be delivered in the future depends on share value at maturity of the contract, if exercised. Alternatively, the contract can be cash settled.

Example 3-1 Prepaid Variable Forward

An investor with a share price at $125 enters a prepaid variable forward agreement that pays him $110 immediately in exchange for a variable number of shares in a few years. The variability hinges on a long put and a short call with strike prices of $120 and $135, respectively. If the price of the shares is less than $120 in three years, the owner would be required to deliver all his shares. Between $120 and $135, the owner delivers $120 worth of shares. Above $135, the owner delivers $120 worth of shares plus the value above $135.

Alternatively, if the share value is less than $120 at maturity, the owner may pay the dealer the actual share value in cash. If the share price is between $120 and $135, the owner pays the dealer $120 in cash. If the price is greater than $135 per share, the owner pays the dealer $120 plus the difference above $135 in cash.

In reality, a collar may be highly scrutinized by the tax authorities, especially for HNW clients. The hedge should be structured to avoid eliminating all economic incentives and disincentives of the concentrated position.

A key tax issue called *mismatch in character* arises when gains (losses) on the underlying and losses (gains) on the hedge cannot be used to offset each other. An example would be exercise of employee stock options granted as compensation, which will generate gains treated like ordinary income, but trying to offset it with a derivatives-based hedge that will result in capital losses. The capital losses cannot be used to offset ordinary income and will be lost unless the employee has other capital gains.

Yield Enhancement

Writing covered calls against some or all of the shares can increase the return to an owner of a concentrated position. The share owner receives the call premium, and continues to receive distributions associated with share ownership. The owner has continued exposure to any potential downside on the share price, and has capped appreciation to the strike price plus the premium received. This strategy works best if the owner believes the share price will stay in a trading range through call expiration. That way, there is little downside risk and the owner will keep the call premium when they expire unexercised. One of the great benefits may be that owners become psychologically invested in the idea of eventually disposing of the shares.

Tax-Optimized Equity Strategies

Tax-optimized equity strategies start with the idea of tax efficiency and incorporate risk and return dimensions:

- *Index tracking separately managed portfolios*—The owner sells or monetizes part of the concentrated position and purchases assets that closely follow an index (e.g., the S&P 500) but outperform it on an after-tax basis.
- *Completeness portfolios*—Offsets the risk of the concentrated position such that the net risk tracks a broad market benchmark such as the S&P 500, often by avoiding similar industry exposure.

Both strategies use gain deferral and opportunistic tax-loss harvesting to offset tax liability from additional sale of the concentrated position, which can then be invested in the strategy. The completeness portfolio eventually becomes an index-tracking portfolio while either strategy will eventually diminish the concentrated position. These do not necessarily lessen downside from systematic risk, however, and may certainly create tax liability as positions within the portfolios appreciate.

Cross Hedging

Cross-hedging an underlying asset with a derivative against a different underlying asset may work in situations where the underlying has no market-based derivative. For example, shares in a privately held company will not have put and call options available. In that case, a derivative against another highly correlated asset may suffice. While this hedges market risk, it does not hedge asset-specific risk. Therefore, owners should avoid strategies that leave them exposed to significant asset-specific downside risk such as short positions and cashless collars. Puts may still have a valuable strategic benefit.

Exchange Funds

An *exchange fund* is a partnership in which the forming partners have contributed low-basis concentrated positions. Each partner then holds a pro-rata partnership interest in a more diversified pool of assets. Partners must remain in the pool for seven years to satisfy tax law requirements in the U.S., at which time they have the option to continue investment in the fund or receive a basket of securities from the pool equal to their partnership value. Their cost basis remains the value of the securities originally contributed to the pool. Note that the exchange fund does not fully eliminate future taxes but defers them.

LESSON 4: MANAGING THE RISK OF PRIVATE BUSINESS EQUITY

LOS 13j: Describe strategies for managing concentrated positions in privately held businesses. Vol 2, pp 356–366

LOS 13l: Evaluate and recommend techniques for tax efficiently managing the risks of concentrated positions in publicly traded common stock, privately held businesses, and real estate. Vol 2, pp 356–366

Private Equity

In addition to being asset rich and cash poor, business owners may have considerations related to selling a business, such as management requirements, business aptitude of heirs, etc. Existing shareholders may have little or no equity and may be prevented from selling to outsiders. Generating liquidity often results in dilution or even loss of control.

Typical Profile

The business, usually between $10 and $500 million, is often a source of pride and income for many business owners. It comprises the bulk of a typical client's net worth, and real estate may be heavily represented in its assets. Owner personalities may differ widely, but they typically have inter-dependent business and personal lives, often with close friends or family members running various aspects of the business.

Business owners overestimate the value of the business and underestimate the risks inherent in such a concentrated position. Aside from old age, it may take illness, offers from competition, or knowledge that an heir has no interest in running the business to cause serious consideration of an exit plan.

Monetization Strategies

A business owner who finally reaches out for financial advice may be unaware of the tax liabilities and, if aware, is unaware of the strategies for monetizing the business in a tax-favorable way. Most incorrectly assume it to be a one-time hold or sell decision. In many cases, however, the optimal strategy may be implemented to decrease asset concentration and improve liquidity over several years, based on market factors and tax laws at any particular time.

Sale or Gifting

A business owner's most favorable purchase offer will come from a *strategic buyer* who can realize significant synergies from the firm. This may include not only increasing revenue and improving the cost structure of the combined firms, but also in realizing entry to markets that may otherwise be closed, or in acquiring a product that rounds out an existing line. Strategic buyers will often pay a premium over asset value, or even over ongoing business value.

A *financial buyer*, however, will often be willing to pay less because they do not have synergistic opportunities from which to recoup a premium. Private equity firms, for example, often purchase such private companies from a pool of assets and target a high internal rate of return over 3–5 years. At the end of the holding period, financial buyers will have optimized the business and can reap the rewards from selling to a strategic buyer.

A partial sale, or *divestiture*, usually involves non-core assets (i.e., those not necessary for running the company's core business). Such non-core assets may include land that has a highest and best use in an alternative outside the company, or business assets in a division which no longer fit the company's strategic plans.

While family members may not have the capital to purchase the business or divested assets, the owner may be able to accomplish this through tax-advantaged gifting strategies or bequests. Gifting, however, may not leave the owner sufficient capital if funds outside the concentrated position are not available.

Management Buyout (MBO)

A *management buyout* (MBO) involves purchase of the firm by senior managers and other key employees. Senior managers and key employees may lack independent entrepreneurial reputations, however, and find it difficult to find financing for the buyout. As a result, purchase offers will generally be less than from a third party, with the divesting entrepreneur asked to accept a promissory note with a significant portion deferred and contingent upon financial performance. At some point the entrepreneur may even have to step back into the business to once again run it.

The owner who has attempted to sell the company prior to the MBO option may also find the employees somewhat hostile to deal with. Therefore, owners should consider MBOs only if they offer a better purchase price than third-party buyers and not as a concession to formerly loyal employees.

Recapitalization

Business owners not yet ready to give up management may instead choose *leveraged recapitalization* of the business using outside equity from a private equity capital firm, along with subordinated debt that may also be arranged or provided by the same firm. The owner typically sells 60–80% of the firm, and retains enough interest to continue growing it. The owner then invests the after-tax proceeds into a diversified portfolio.

The owner does cede overall control of the firm, but maintains management authority, a position in the community, and continues to polish the reputation of being a shrewd business person.

Credit Secured by Company Shares

This method avoids a taxable event if structured correctly because it does not sell stock or issue a dividend. Instead, the company borrows money that it loans to the share owner. In many cases, the company offers a put to the lender against the owner's shares for security against the loan. The company can fund the put obligation, if exercised, through its existing debt arrangements or through a special letter of credit for the purpose. If the lender exercises the put, it would trigger a taxable sale of the stock. Of course, the borrower must at some point repay the loan. In the interim, however, the owner maintains control, has use of the money, and can deduct the interest expense.

Initial Public Offering

Although the costs of an IPO (i.e., "going public") are high, the share price offered to the market compensates for that cost. In addition, the investor will lose a good bit of the authority, privacy, and autonomy of running a private company. This can be useful if the investor intends to remain involved in the company for the near future, but not if the owner intends to exit the company entirely.

Employee Stock Ownership Plan

The U.S., for example, has allowed owners to sell their shares to a type of qualified pension plan known as an *employee stock ownership plan* (ESOP). In a *leveraged ESOP*, the company borrows money to fund the purchase. The owner selling shares in a so-called subchapter C firm enjoys deferred capital gains taxes (and a potential step-up in basis for the heirs) on the offered shares. By offering an increasing number of shares over time, the owner participates in the potential upside while gradually withdrawing from a control position in a tax-advantaged manner. Setup and maintenance fees can be high.

Strategy Evaluation

The combined goals of divestment value and tax minimization can combine to determine the best after-tax outcome. For example, selling to a private equity firm will have a different initial net value, and the consequent tax on various strategies will lead to a different after-tax outcome. In some cases, the seller and buyer span the difference between their presumed valuations by means of an *earnout*, in which the owner receives an additional payment if the company meets pre-established targets after conclusion of the sale. Various other methods of disposition delay an owner's receipt of the full purchase price. In some cases, the owner may agree to lend all or part of the money necessary to close the deal.

Example 4-1

The 100% owner of a private company wishes to monetize his position while retaining control until his death. He has two offers on the table: 1) An all cash proposal for $500 million in exchange for all his shares, or 2) $550 million in shares (i.e., no cash) from a large, diversified conglomerate. He does not wish to bear the risk of holding $500 million in the conglomerate's shares, and has learned he will be able to monetize 99% via a short against the box strategy that costs 30 basis points annually. He has essentially zero basis in the shares and is subject to a capital gains tax rate of 25%. His advisor on the transactions has indicated he can defer the capital gains tax by exchanging shares. At death, the bequest of shares will occur at a stepped-up basis such that neither he nor his heirs will be subject to gains tax. The owner will generate the *greatest* net after-tax proceeds from the:

    A.   all cash proposal.
    B.   stock swap with immediate sale.
    C.   stock swap with short against the box.

Solution:

    C.   The all cash proposal will have an after-tax value of $375 million [$500 million × (1 − 0.25)]. The swap and immediate sale will net $412.5 million [$550 million × (1 − 0.25)]. The short against the box strategy will result in $544.5 million ($550 million × 0.99), but will cost $1.63 million ($550 million × 0.99 × 0.0030) annually to maintain. The difference in the second and third strategies is essentially equivalent to 81 years of paying the $1.63 million, so even considering the present value of that cost he is better off with the third strategy. Plus, he maintains a control position.

LESSON 5: MANAGING THE RISK OF INVESTMENT IN REAL ESTATE

LOS 13k: Describe strategies for managing concentrated positions in real estate. Vol 2, pp 366–369

LOS 13l: Evaluate and recommend techniques for tax efficiently managing the risks of concentrated positions in publicly traded common stock, privately held businesses, and real estate. Vol 2, pp 366–369

INVESTMENT REAL ESTATE

Real estate may be owned by a closely held company or as a separate investment, but often represents a concentrated position within the HNW individual's portfolio. Real estate owners have a tendency to underestimate the risks of their concentrated position and overestimate the value of their investment. However, a long-term position will typically have a substantial embedded gain that may be triggered by attempting to cash out of or monetize the position.

A business or investment rationale should drive the sale or monetization decision rather than solely basing such a decision on taxes. If a solid reason exists, then minimizing taxes may drive the selection of method. Other than selling the property, several monetization techniques may be available.

Sale and Leaseback

Sale and leaseback frees owner equity (or can raise capital) while allowing the owner to continue using the property. The advantage is that the owner can realize 100% of the value immediately (versus the loan-to-value amount of a refinance) less any debt. Any debt associated with the real estate will be cleared from the balance sheet. Rental payments are also fully deductible versus the interest deductibility of a mortgage loan.

Mortgage Refinance

A *mortgage refinance* allows the property owner to take out a new mortgage against the presumably appreciated property, extinguish any underlying mortgage, and enjoy the proceeds without tax consequences. The owner will continue to benefit from additional appreciation over time. The downside is that mortgage lenders typically require loan-to-value ratios of only 70–90 percent of appraised value. However, investors may be able to structure the loan such that the cash flow from owning the property offsets the mortgage payment.

If default on the loan may only be satisfied by a lender through foreclosure of the property and not against the borrower's other assets (i.e., a *non-recourse loan)*, the borrower has reduced investment concentration via the equivalent of a put issued by the lender for the loan amount, and monetized that amount of the property.

Example 5-1

A business owner personally owns a $10 million, fully-depreciated property used by his privately-held company, but it is not strategically important. The owner can sell the property for $10 million and his business can lease it back. Alternatively, the owner can refinance the property with 70% LTV. The owner has $2.5 million in capital losses carried forward for personal use, and the transaction will be subject to a 25% capital gains tax. The amount the owner will realize from sale and leaseback compared to refinance is *closest* to:

    A. $7.5 million.
    B. $10.0 million.
    C. $12.5 million.

Solution:

    B.   The owner will realize only $7 million ($10mm × 0.70) through refinance, but will immediately realize $10 million. His $2.5 million capital gains tax liability will be offset against his losses carried forward.

Charitable Giving

A U.S. investor may be able to donate property (especially property with limited appreciation potential) to a donor-advised fund for a charitable organization, which may then keep the property or sell it to provide funds for a diversified portfolio. The donor may receive a tax deduction equal to fair market value of the property under certain circumstances, while the charity's sale and reinvestment will permanently escape depreciation recapture, capital gains tax, and tax on future earnings. A tax-exempt charitable trust provides the same function under most common law jurisdictions.

Other Techniques

Although outside the scope of this treatment, it is possible to structure a monetizing tax-free exchange in which the property owner exchanges his assets for other assets of equal value. This can allow the property owner to immediately hedge risk of a concentrated position and ultimately eliminate the capital gains tax that would be due on the original property.

Other techniques include:

- Joint venture;
- Conversion to condominium; and
- Selling the building while maintaining control through a long-term ground lease.

READING 14: RISK MANAGEMENT FOR INDIVIDUALS

Time to complete: 3 or more hours

Reading Summary: The reading emphasizes an economic (or holistic) balance sheet presenting traditional assets and liabilities as well as recognizing the present value of future assets and liabilities, with the most significant asset being human capital. Risks to the balance sheet can be managed or, alternatively, transferred by using various insurance products.

LESSON 1: HUMAN CAPITAL AND FINANCIAL CAPITAL

LOS 14a: Compare the characteristics of human capital and financial capital as components of an individual's total wealth. Vol 2, pp 382–390

The two primary components of an individual's wealth can be described as:

1. **Human capital:** This is the present value of the individual's future expected labor income. The goal is to view human capital as its own asset with risk and return characteristics.
2. **Financial capital:** This consists of bank accounts, individual securities, pooled funds, retirement accounts, the family home, and any other assets owned by the individual that are not considered human capital.

Like other assets, the present value of human capital is determined by discounting expected future earnings by an appropriate discount rate. Professions with stable growth of future earnings would have a low discount rate to reflect low risk—for example, government employees, teachers, and professors. Use a higher discount rate for professions with higher-risk cash flows—for example, investment bankers and race car drivers. All else held equal, two individuals with the same expected salary can have different human capital because of differences in the riskiness of their earnings and discount rates.

> For most young investors, human capital can represent a sizable part of total wealth. Think about how to calculate the present value of your own human capital. This will help you remember the process for the exam.

Anybody who is not currently retired has human capital. When an individual retires, human capital decreases to zero.

Human capital is calculated as follows:

$$HC_0 = \sum_{t=1}^{N} \frac{p(s_t)w_{t-1}(1+g_t)}{(1+r_f+y)^t}$$

> The volatility of an individual's earnings will determine whether to use a high or low discount rate.

Example 1-1 demonstrates how to calculate the present value of human capital for an individual who is 60 years old and plans on retiring in 5 years.

Example 1-1: Estimating the Present Value of Human Capital

Example from Volume 2, CFA Curriculum 2017

Using Equation 1, we briefly demonstrate how to estimate the present value of an individual's human capital. John Adam is 60 years old and plans on retiring in 5 years. Adam's annual wage is currently $50,000 and is expected to grow 2% per year. The risk-free rate is 4%. Adam works in a job with a moderate degree of occupational risk; therefore, we assume a risk adjustment based on occupational income volatility of 3%. There is a 99% probability that Adam survives the first year, a 98% probability that he survives the second year, and probabilities of 98%, 97%, and 96% for the following years, respectively. Given this information and using Equation 2, what is the present value of Adam's human capital?

Wage growth rate	= 2%
Risk-free rate	= 4%
Income volatility adjustment	= 3%
Total discount rate	= 7%

Year	Wages (2% annual growth)	Present Value of Wages[a]	Probability of Survival	Probability-Weighted Wages[b]
1	$51,000	$47,664	99%	$47,187
2	$52,020	$45,436	98%	$44,527
3	$53,060	$43,313	98%	$42,447
4	$54,122	$41,289	97%	$40,050
5	$55,204	$39,360	96%	$37,786
	Total value of human capital			$211,997

[a] This column illustrates wages discounted by 7% as indicated by the discount rate shown. For example: $47,664 = $51,000/1.07; $45,436 = $52,020/1.07^2; and so on.
[b] The calculation for this column is as follows: $47,187 = $47,664 × 99%. A similar calculation is used for the following years.

LESSON 2: SEVEN FINANCIAL STAGES OF LIFE

LOS 14c: Discuss the financial stages of life for an individual.
Vol 2, pp 391–394

Table 2-1 categorizes the financial stages of life for adults into seven periods, which follow the order as a person ages.

Table 2-1: Seven Financial Stages of Life

Stage Name	Description and Age Range	Key Characteristics	Financial Advisor Can Help With…
Education phase	Investing in knowledge through formal education or skill development	Financially dependent on parents Very little financial capital Almost no focus on savings or risk management	Those with dependents might need life insurance.
Early career	Completes education and enters workforce (age 18 to 20s or early 30s)	Gets married, has children, buys home High family and housing expenses may not allow for retirement savings	Life insurance can supplement lack of sufficient financial and human capital.
Career development	Specific skill development within a given field (age 35 to 50)	Accumulation for children's college education Large purchases such as vacation home, travel	Retirement saving
Peak accumulation	Moving toward maximum earnings and greatest opportunity for wealth accumulation (age 51 to 60)	Retirement planning and travel High career risk as high-paying job might not be replaced	Reducing investment risk Developing retirement income strategies
Pre-retirement	A few years before planned retirement age	Income often at career highs	Decreasing investment risk Tax planning for retirement distributions
Early retirement	Period of comfortable income and enough assets to cover living expenses (at least first 10 years of retirement)	Use savings for enjoyment Most active period of retirement Less likely to suffer from cognitive or mobility impairments	Still a need for asset growth as this phase could last 20 years
Late retirement	Unknown duration	Physical activity declines Cognitive or physical problems may deplete savings May need long-term health care	Annuities to reduce or eliminate longevity risk

The exam may require you to select the financial stage name appropriate to the description of a particular client. A constructed response or other template-type question in the morning session could be worth as many as 6 to 9 points. Try thinking about where you are in one of the seven stages to recall at least one of them on the exam.

LESSON 3: A FRAMEWORK FOR INDIVIDUAL RISK MANAGEMENT

LOS 14b: Discuss the relationships among human capital, financial capital, and net wealth. Vol 2, pp 394–400

LOS 14d: Discuss an economic (holistic) balance sheet. Vol 2, pp 394–400

Risk management for individuals involves identifying risks to household assets and well-being and to develop an appropriate strategy to deal with those risks. The four key steps in the risk management process are:

1. **Specify the objective:** The goal is to maximize household welfare through a balance of risk taking and safety. Individuals need to decide how much risk they are willing to take to satisfy long-term spending goals.
2. **Identify risks:** There are six risks (earnings, premature death, longevity, property, liability, and health), discussed later.
3. **Evaluate risks and select appropriate methods to manage the risks:** Methods include *risk avoidance* by not engaging in the risky activity; *risk reduction* by lowering the likelihood that a risk will occur or decreasing the severity of the loss; *risk transfer* through the purchase of insurance and annuities; and *risk retention (or self-insuring)* by keeping the risk and setting aside money to cover potential losses.
4. **Monitor outcomes and risk exposures and make appropriate adjustments in methods:** Review the client's risk management plan at major life changes such as the birth of a new child, marriage, inheritance, and so on.

An economic (holistic) balance sheet depicts an individual's overall financial health by accounting for the present value of all available marketable and non-marketable assets and liabilities, as shown in Table 3-1.

Table 3-1: Economic (Holistic) Balance Sheet

Assets		Liabilities	
Financial capital		Debt	
Liquid assets	$275,000	Credit card debt	$15,000
Investment assets	$1,265,000	Car loan	$35,000
Personal property	$2,150,000	Home mortgage	$685,000
Subtotal	$3,690,000	Home equity loan	$60,000
		Subtotal	$795,000
Human capital	$1,800,000	Lifetime consumption needs	$3,500,000
Pension value	$250,000	Bequests	$300,000
Total assets	**$5,740,000**	**Total liabilities**	**$4,595,000**
		Net wealth	**$1,145,000**

A traditional balance sheet using marketable assets and liabilities from Table 3-1 that exist today would include the following items:

- **Financial capital:** Includes liquid assets (checking accounts, certificates of deposit); investment assets (taxable, non-taxable, vested portion of retirement plans, cash value of life insurance); and personal property (house, car, and house contents). In Table 3-1, the total amount of financial capital is $3,690,000.
- **Debt:** Includes short-term liabilities (credit card debt) and long-term liabilities (car loan, home mortgage, and home equity loan). In Table 3-1, the total amount of debt is $795,000.
- **Net worth:** Represents the difference between financial capital and debt. In Table 3-1, net worth is equal to $2,895,000.

The holistic (economic) balance sheet includes the present value of non-marketable human capital and non-vested pensions (assets), and the present value of lifetime consumption and bequests (liabilities) that can be considered part of the investor's net wealth. In Table 3-1, we have shaded those items to distinguish them from financial capital and debt. Net wealth is equal to the economic assets minus economic liabilities, which in Table 3-1 is equal to $1,145,000. A holistic (economic) balance sheet provides a more accurate framework to maximize utility of future consumption.

In general, a young family will have a high percentage of economic assets in human capital and, as the household ages, the weight of human capital will decrease and the weight of tangible financial assets will increase. Financial capital tends to be greatest when an individual first retires.

> In this reading, be careful not to confuse net worth and net wealth. They are different measures.

The weight of the present value of vested employer-sponsored pensions generally increases later in the life cycle. The formula for calculating the present value of a mortality-weighted pension is:

$$mNPV_0 = \sum_{t=1}^{N} \frac{p(s_t)b_t}{(1+r)^t}$$

where:
b_t = the future expected vested benefit
$[p(s_t)]$ = the probability of surviving until year t
r = a discount rate

Note that this formula looks similar to the one for human capital, but without the occupational income volatility variable in the denominator. When determining the most appropriate discount rate to use for vested employer pensions, consider the following three items:

1. **Plan's financial health, such as its funded status:** We would use a lower discount rate for income from plans with a fund surplus compared to plans with a fund deficit.
2. **Credit quality of the sponsoring company:** If the company has issued long-term bonds, the yield can serve as a proxy for the discount rate.
3. **Additional credit support:** In some countries, the government offers a guarantee in case a local defined-benefit pension plan becomes insolvent.

These points are for a defined-benefit (DB) pension plan sponsored by a corporation. For government-sponsored pensions, it is important to also consider the financial health of the sponsoring government (e.g., watch for increasing or decreasing debt levels) as well as political risk at the country level.

LOS 14e: Discuss risks (earnings, premature death, longevity, property, liability, and health risks) in relation to human and financial capital. Vol 2, pp 400–405

The six risks to human and financial capital are:

1. **Earnings risk:** Related to events that could negatively affect someone's human and financial capital, such as health issues, losing a job in an economically depressed area, or working for a company that is tied to the swings in the business cycle. Earnings risk through the loss of a job can affect the value of financial capital as well as human capital through lower future salaries, higher discount rates, or both. *We will discuss how to protect against earnings risk related to injury with disability insurance later.*

2. **Premature death (mortality risk):** Death of an individual, such as a family member, whose future earnings (human capital) were expected to help pay for the financial needs and goals of the household. The present value of expected services provided by that person as well as death expenses related to funeral and burial should also be considered. *We will discuss how to protect against premature death risk with life insurance later.*

3. **Longevity risk:** Reaching an age at which one's income and financial assets are insufficient to provide adequate support. This relates to an extended retirement period that results from living longer than expected. A person concerned about outliving his or her assets can continue working to an older retirement age. *We will also discuss how to protect against longevity risk with annuities later.*

4. **Property risk:** The possibility that one's property may be damaged, destroyed, stolen, or lost. Loss of property is associated with a loss of financial capital. We will discuss how to protect against property risk with homeowner's insurance later.

5. **Liability risk:** The possibility of legal liability for the financial costs of property damage or physical injury such as being in an auto accident or a guest being harmed in your home. *We will discuss how to protect against liability risk with liability insurance later.*

6. **Health risk:** Illness or injury that results in costs such as coinsurance, copayments, and deductibles relating to diagnostics, treatments, and procedures. Illness and injury can also affect the individual's future earnings ability, which will reduce human capital. Risks of long-term health care can be considered both a health risk and longevity risk. *We will discuss how to protect against health risk with health insurance later.*

LESSON 4: LIFE INSURANCE

LOS 14f: Describe types of insurance relevant to personal financial planning. Vol 2, pp 405–416

The primary purpose of life insurance is to help replace the economic value of an individual to a family or a business in the event of that individual's death. The family's need for life insurance is related to the potential loss associated with the future earnings power of that individual.

There are two types of life insurance:

1. **Temporary life insurance:** Insurance for a certain period of time specified at purchase, known as a term. If the individual survives for the entire term, say 20 years, then the policy will terminate unless it automatically renews. Premiums can either remain fixed (or level) or increase over the term as the mortality risk increases. *There is no cash value for term life insurance.*
2. **Permanent insurance:** Lifetime coverage, assuming the premiums are paid over the entire period. Policy premiums are fixed, and there is generally a cash value associated with the policy. There are two basic types of permanent insurance: whole life and universal life. Whole life remains in force for the entire life of the insured. Universal life has more flexibility than whole life to vary the face amount of insurance, pay higher or lower premiums, and invest the cash value.

Both types of insurance are deemed **non-cancelable**; the policy only lapses at the end of the term (for temporary insurance) or upon death (for permanent insurance), provided that the premiums have been paid.

Here are some more general terms mainly related to permanent insurance that you need to be familiar with:

1. **Participating/non-participating:** Participating allows for the cash value to grow at a higher rate than the guaranteed value based on the profits of the insurance company. Fixed growth values are known as non-participating.
2. **Non-forfeiture clause:** A policyholder has the option to receive a portion of benefits if premium payments are missed and the policy lapses. There are three options: cash surrender option, where the cash value is paid; paid-up option, where the cash value is used to purchase a single-premium whole life policy; and extended term option, where the cash value is used to purchase a term life policy, usually with the same face value as the previous policy.
3. **Riders:** Riders provide protection beyond the basic policy or other modification to a basic policy provision. One example is accidental death and dismemberment (AD&D), which increases the payout if/when the insured dies or is dismembered by an accident. Other common riders include accelerated death benefit, where those who are terminally ill can receive the death benefits while still alive; guaranteed insurability, which allows the policyholder to buy more insurance later at predefined periods; and waiver of premium, where future premiums are waived if the insured becomes disabled.
4. **Viatical settlement:** These allow the policyholder to sell the policy to a third party. After buying the policy, the third party is responsible for paying premiums and will receive the death benefit when the insured dies.

LOS 14g: Describe the basic elements of a life insurance policy and how insurers price a life insurance policy. Vol 2, pp 417–422

The basic elements of a life insurance policy include:

- **Term and type of insurance:** For example, 30-year temporary life policy.
- **Amount of benefits:** For example, $250,000.
- **Limitations under which death benefit could be withheld:** These could include suicide of the insured within two years after purchasing the policy, or if the insured made material misrepresentations during the application process.
- **Contestability period:** The period when the insurance company can investigate and deny claims.
- **Premium schedule:** Specifying the amount and frequency of premiums to be paid to the insurance company.
- **Riders:** Modifications to basic coverage (see previous points).

There are four parties involved in every life insurance policy, which are also considered basic elements:

1. **Insured:** The person whose death triggers the death benefit payment.
2. **Policy owner:** Owns the policy and is responsible for paying premiums. In most policies, the insured and the policy owner are the same person. When the insured is not the policy owner, the owner must have an insurable interest in the life of the insured. Examples of insurable interests include an ex-spouse purchasing insurance on the other ex-spouse following a divorce to cover future spousal or child-support payments or a company purchasing insurance on a key executive.
3. **Beneficiary (or beneficiaries):** Receives the death benefit, either as a lump sum (more common) or an annuity (less common).
4. **Insurer:** The insurance company that writes the policy and pays the death benefits to the beneficiary when the insured dies.

Note that the insurance company will require the owner to have a reason for taking out the policy (i.e., insurable interest) other than to gamble on the insured's death.

There are three main considerations in pricing a life insurance policy:

1. **Mortality expectations:** Probability that the insured will die during the term of the policy, as shown in Table 4-1. Actuaries rely on historical data and future mortality expectations based on age, gender, and other significant medical conditions, such as smoking/non-smoking. During the underwriting process, actuaries make adjustments to the mortality tables to recognize other factors such as family disease history, risky hobbies, and so forth. All else held equal, men live shorter lives than women, and given the same age, a man is expected to pay more for life insurance.
2. **Discount rate (or interest factor):** Represents the insurance company's assumed rate of return on its investment portfolio.
3. **Loading:** Life insurance company expenses and profits, if any, discussed later.

Underwriting is the term used when an insurance company assumes the risks that the individual wishes to transfer to the insurance company in exchange for a premium.

Table 4-1: Mortality of Males and Females at Certain Ages[1]

	Male			Female		
Age	Composite	Non-Smoker	Smoker	Composite	Non-Smoker	Smoker
20	0.10%	0.10%	0.13%	0.05%	0.05%	0.06%
25	0.11	0.10	0.16	0.05	0.05	0.08
30	0.11	0.10	0.18	0.07	0.06	0.10
35	0.12	0.11	0.20	0.10	0.09	0.15
40	0.17	0.15	0.28	0.13	0.12	0.21
45	0.27	0.23	0.46	0.19	0.17	0.31
50	0.38	0.33	0.65	0.31	0.28	0.54
55	0.62	0.55	1.06	0.51	0.47	0.91
60	0.99	0.89	1.63	0.80	0.74	1.40
65	1.69	1.55	2.66	1.19	1.11	2.03
70	2.58	2.41	3.79	1.78	1.68	2.98
75	4.19	4.00	5.73	2.79	2.66	4.52
80	7.01	6.79	9.01	4.39	4.24	6.70
85	11.66	11.41	14.01	7.45	7.28	10.54

Using information from Table 4-1, the one-year mortality rate of a 35-year-old, nonsmoking male is 0.11%. This means that there is a 0.11% probability that this person will die before the age of 36. If this individual purchases $100,000 worth of life insurance, the expected outflow to the insurance company at the end of the year is equal to:

Expected outflow to the insurance company = [One-year mortality rate × Amount of death benefit + (One-year mortality rate) × $0]

Expected outflow to the insurance company = 0.0011 × $100,000 + 0.9989 × $0

Expected outflow to the insurance company = $110.00

Mortality expectations, the expected outflow to the insurance company, and the discount rate are used to calculate the *net premium*. Now that we have the expected outflow, if we assume that the insurance company can earn a 6% expected return on its investment portfolio, the net premium equals:

Net premium = Expected outflow to the insurance company/(1 + Expected return on the investment portfolio)

Net premium = $110.00/1.06 = $103.77

> Even though the mortality table has age increments of five years, the mortality rates are for one year.

The *gross premium* equals the net premium plus a *load* representing costs to the life insurance company:

1. **Underwriting costs:** Sales commission to the agent who sold the commission plus the cost of a physical exam, if required.

2. **Ongoing expenses:** Overhead and administration expenses, monitoring the policy, and verifying death claims. Renewal commissions are paid to the selling agent for the first years of the policy as an incentive to provide advice to the policyholder and to discourage the policy owner from terminating the policy.

The load may also include a profit based on the type of life insurance company:

1. **Stock companies:** These are owned by shareholders and have a profit motive, so they add a projected profit to the load.
2. **Mutual companies:** These are owned by the policyholders themselves, so there is no profit motive, although the gross premium is typically higher than the net premium plus expenses. If mortality outcomes and investment returns are more favorable than expected, the policyholders receive a non-taxable return of their premium equal to the difference between the gross premium and net premium plus expenses.

Policyholders have a choice when deciding the term to purchase. Annual renewable (one-year) policies for a new insured at a particular age have lower annual premiums than longer-term policies, such as 20 years, which must average out the higher mortality charges in later years. Insurance companies offer loss leaders (i.e., low initial rates) on annually renewable insurance, with policyholders switching to other companies at the end of the short term. However, illness or an accident could cause the renewed policy to be much more expensive.

Whole life policies offer level premiums and the prospect of accumulation of cash value within the policy. The cash value can be withdrawn when the policy endows (matures) or when the policy is terminated by the policyholder. The cash value can also be borrowed as a loan while keeping the life insurance component of the policy in force, but the loan remains a liability that must be subtracted from any death benefit paid. Cash values increase slowly in the early years of the whole life policy as the insurance company makes up for its underwriting expenses. The insurance company is required by regulators to maintain a policy reserve, which is a liability for the company, in the amount of the cash value to be paid out to the insureds if they have not died by the time it is due to be paid.

Paying premiums to an insurance company to assume mortality risk reduces lifetime wealth.

The premium and the face value of the whole life policy remain constant, and the cash value increases, but the insurance value decreases over time. This tends to follow the typical pattern of requiring less life insurance as a person gets older and the need to protect human capital diminishes. Remember, human capital tends to fall toward zero as an individual reaches retirement.

When thinking about the cost of life insurance, there is more to consider than just choosing the policy with the lowest premium. There are many variables at play, and it is not easy for potential consumers to compare the cost of life insurance policies. However, there are two methods used to compare the prices of whole life insurance policies:

1. **Net payment cost index:** This assumes that the insured person will die at the end of a specified period, such as 20 years.
2. **Surrender cost index:** This assumes that the policy will be surrendered at the end of the period and that the policyholder will receive the projected cash value.

We will demonstrate how these two indexes are calculated using the following client and product information (see Tables 4-2 and 4-3):

- Face value of the whole life policy: $100,000
- Number of annual periods: 20
- Annual premium of $2,000 paid at the beginning of the year
- Policy dividends: $500, paid at the end of the year
- Cash value: $22,500 projected for the end of Year 20

Table 4-2: Net Payment Cost Index Calculation[2]

Future value of premiums (annuity due): US$2,000 annual payment, 20 years, 5%	US$69,439
Future value of dividends (ordinary annuity): US$500 annual payment, 20 years, 5%	−16,533
20-year insurance cost	US$52,906
Annual payments for 20-year insurance cost (annuity due): 20 years, 5%	1,524
Divide by US$ thousands of face value	÷100
Net Payment Cost Index, cost per US$ thousand per year	US$15.24

Table 4-3: Surrender Cost Index Calculation[3]

Future value of premiums (annuity due): US$2,000 annual payment, 20 years, 5%	US$69,439
Future value of dividends (ordinary annuity): US$500 annual payment, 20 years, 5%	−16,533
20-year cash value (given above)	−22,500
20-year insurance cost	US$30,406
Annual payments for 20-year insurance cost (annuity due): 20 years, 5%	876
Divide by US$ thousands of face value	÷100
Surrender Cost Index, cost per US$ thousand per year	US$8.76

> Surrender cost calculations are included here because they would make ideal problem-solving questions on the CFA exam. Be able to calculate the surrender cost index and interpret it in terms of value relative to other policies.

Surrender cost index indicates the annual cost of accumulating cash during the assumed holding period (i.e., 20 years in this case). Companies with lower index value are more efficient at delivering surrender value.

---

2 - Net Payment Cost Index Calculation, Volume 2, CFA Curriculum 2019
3 - Surrender Cost Index Calculation, Volume 2, CFA Curriculum 2019

LESSON 5: OTHER TYPES OF INSURANCE

LOS 14f: Describe types of insurance relevant to personal financial planning. Vol 2, pp 405–416

Disability Income Insurance

Disability income insurance is designed to reduce earnings risk caused by injury or disability that results in the insured becoming less than fully employed. Disabilities tend to be for short periods of time rather than for life.

There are three definitions of full disability that address inability to perform the duties of:

1. One's regular occupation
2. Any occupation for which one is suited by education and experience
3. Any occupation

Using the first definition, a surgeon who loses the use of his or her dominant hand is deemed to be disabled. Using the second definition, a surgeon able to perform the duties of a general practitioner would not be deemed disabled. Using the third definition, even if the surgeon could not practice as a doctor but could teach at a medical school (or any other occupation), he or she would not be deemed disabled. *For professionals with highly specialized skills, insurance contracts that include the first definition provide the most inclusive coverage, though they will have more expensive premiums.*

As an extension to the definition of fully disabled, partial disability means that although the insured cannot perform all of the duties of his or her profession, the individual can remain employed at a lower income. Residual disability means that the insured can perform all professional duties, but the individual cannot earn as much money after the disability.

Premiums tend to be fixed, are based on the age of the insured, and are underwritten based on the health and occupation of the insured. Coverage is through individual policies and through many employers. Disabled individuals will receive a percentage of the difference between their pre- and post-injury income, usually 60% to 80%, because other pre-injury expenses will be lower (such as commuting to work) and to reduce the likelihood of fraudulent claims.

Additional contract terms include:

- **Benefit period:** How long the payments will be made, typically until retirement. Usually, a minimum number of years of benefits is specified, such as five years, to encourage those close to retirement to maintain their policies.
- **Elimination period (waiting period):** The number of days that the insured must be disabled before payments begin. The typical elimination period in the United States is 90 days. The shorter the elimination period, the higher the premium.
- **Rehabilitation clause:** This clause provides benefits for physical therapy to get the insured back to work as quickly as possible.
- **Waiver of premium:** The policy owner may suspend premiums during a disability period, and premiums paid during the elimination period are returned.

- **Option to purchase additional insurance rider:** The policy owner may increase coverage without further proof of insurability.
- **Cost of living rider:** Benefits will be increased by an accepted cost of living index or some specified percentage each year.
- **Non-cancelable and guaranteed renewable:** The insurance company must renew the policy annually provided premiums are paid, and there will be no changes to the premium or promised disability benefits, even if employment income declines.
- **Non-cancelable:** The insurance company must renew the policy annually provided that premiums are paid, but premiums can be increased for the entire underwriting class (although not for one particular individual). This is less expensive than a guaranteed renewable policy, but insurance companies with historical losses are expected to raise their premiums.

HOMEOWNER'S INSURANCE

A homeowner's policy can be specified as:

- **All risks:** All risks are included except those specified as being excluded.
- **Named risks:** Only risks specifically listed are covered by the policy.

The claims can be settled in one of two ways:

1. **Replacement cost:** The benefit pays the amount required to repair or replace an item with a new item of similar quality based on today's prices.
2. **Actual cash value:** The benefit equals replacement cost less depreciation. Clearly, the replacement cost policy will have higher premiums than the actual cash value.

A key part of the insurance policy is the *deductible*, which is the amount that the policyholder must pay before any money is paid by the insurance company. Insurance companies price their policies to encourage the use of a higher deductible so that the policyholder shares more of the risk with the insurance company. A higher deductible means a lower insurance premium. Consider two policy alternatives:

- **Alternative 1:** Policy with a $500 deductible with an annual premium of $3,000.
- **Alternative 2:** Policy with a $1,000 deductible with an annual premium of $2,900.

The lower deductible costs $100 more in annual premium. The purchaser needs to consider whether the additional $100 of premium is worth the additional $500 loss (difference between deductibles). A higher deductible means that the policyholder retains more risk but increases expected wealth over time by paying lower premiums to the insurance company.

In addition to homeowner's insurance to cover the cost of casualty losses, some mortgage lenders require homeowners to have life insurance sufficient to repay the mortgage should the borrower die. As the mortgage balance declines over time, an insurance policy can be purchased with a declining face value and premiums. By contrast, insurance companies want the house to be insured for its full value (less the value of the land, which cannot be lost or destroyed) so that it will receive larger premiums. If a house is underinsured, say less than 80% of its replacement cost, any losses are reimbursed at a lower rate.

Homeowners' liability is also addressed within the insurance policy to cover visitors injured in an accident in the home, but excludes professional and business liability, which may be covered separately.

AUTOMOBILE INSURANCE

Automobile and other vehicle insurance rates are based on the value of the vehicle and are underwritten on the primary driver's age and driving record.

There are two types of coverage:

1. **Collision:** Covers damage from an accident.
2. **Comprehensive:** Covers damage from other causes, such as fire, hail, glass breakage, and theft.

The insurance amount is up to the replacement cost of the automobile with the same make and model in the same condition. If the cost to repair the automobile is greater than its actual cash value, the insurer will most often pay only the cash value. Liability, including injury and property damage, is also included in the policy. Like a homeowner's policy, the automobile policyholder also retains risk through the use of a deductible. Personal watercraft (boats) and trailers might require a separate insurance policy or an endorsement, which is coverage added to an existing policy.

HEALTH/MEDICAL INSURANCE

In the United States, there are three kinds of health insurance:

1. **Indemnity plan:** The insured can go to any medical service provider, but the insured must pay a specified percentage of "reasonable and customary" fees.
2. **Preferred provider organization (PPO):** A PPO is a network of physicians who charge lower prices to individuals within the plan than to individuals who obtain health care on their own.
3. **Health maintenance organization (HMO):** An HMO allows office visits at no or low cost to encourage individuals to seek treatment for minor medical issues before they become serious.

Comprehensive major medical insurance covers most health care expenses, including physician's fees, surgical fees, hospitalization, lab fees, x-rays, and other reasonable and customary diagnostic and treatment expenses.

Other key terms and features that could affect the premiums of health insurance include:

- **Deductible:** The amount that the insured pays before the insurance company pays any benefit.
- **Coinsurance:** The percentage of any expense that the insurance company will pay, typically 80%.
- **Copayments:** Fixed payments that the insured must make for a particular service, such as $250 per doctor office visit.
- **Maximum out-of-pocket expense (stop-loss limit):** Individual and family maximum amount of expenses incurred beyond which the insurance company will pay 100%.

- **Maximum yearly and lifetime benefits:** The maximum amounts that the insurance company will cover within the respective time periods.
- **Preexisting conditions:** Health conditions that the insured had when applying for insurance that the policy may or may not cover.
- **Preadmission certificate:** An approval from the insurance company before a scheduled (non-emergency) hospital visit or treatment.

Liability Insurance

The liability coverage in a homeowner's or an automobile policy may be inadequate to cover a significant accident. In this case, a separate personal umbrella liability insurance policy can be purchased. Consider a situation where an automobile policy provides $300,000 of liability coverage but the insured driver causes $650,000 worth of damage. The umbrella policy would pay the additional $350,000 beyond the automobile policy coverage. Such umbrella policies are relatively inexpensive.

Other forms of insurance include title insurance, which ensures that the ownership of property and real estate is not in doubt. Pseudo-insurance contracts (also known as service contracts) are sold when purchasing an automobile, home appliance, or other costly product to avoid repair costs. They are offered at the time of purchase, so sellers can charge a high rate because buyers have limited opportunity to compare insurance prices. Such contracts often include a deductible.

LESSON 6: ANNUITIES

LOS 14h: Discuss the use of annuities in personal financial planning. Vol 2, pp 422–426

Annuities are designed to protect against longevity risk. In other words, individuals will live for an unknown number of years after retirement and need to even out their spending over an uncertain timeframe. Private annuities can be purchased from insurance companies. Life insurance provides protection if people die too young, whereas annuities protect people from outliving their retirement savings.

Similar to life insurance, there are four parties to an annuity:

1. **Annuitant:** The person who receives the benefits while alive.
2. **Contract owner:** In most cases, the annuitant owns the contract. However, an employer can purchase an annuity for a retiring employee.
3. **Beneficiary (or beneficiaries):** The person who receives benefits when the annuitant dies, provided that the annuity is purchased with a "period certain," which is a minimum guaranteed payment period.
4. **Insurer:** The insurance company that is licensed to sell the annuity.

There are five annuity types, depending on whether the annuity is paid out immediately (single-premium immediate annuity [SPIA]) or is deferred, and whether the underlying investments in the annuity are more bond-like (fixed) or equity-like (variable).

1. **Immediate fixed annuity:** This is the most common type of annuity. The annuitant trades a single lump sum of money today in exchange for a promised income payment for as long as the annuitant is alive. Table 6-1 shows annual payouts for

males, females, and joint lives for an annuity with and without a 10-year period certain. For example, in return for $100,000 to the insurance company, a 60-year-old male annuitant will receive an annual payment of $6,280 (income yield = $6,280/$100,000). Notice that because women live longer than men on average, a 60-year-old woman will receive a smaller annual payment of $5,870. The joint life payment for a couple is even lower at $5,510 because of the longer payout period for the last of the husband or wife to die. Payouts increase with age because of the higher likelihood of death and decrease with the addition of the period certain.

Table 6-1: An Example of Annual Payouts as a Percentage of Initial Premium

	Life Only				Life with 10-Year Period Certain		
Age	Male	Female	Joint	Age	Male	Female	Joint
60	6.28%	5.87%	5.51%	60	6.15%	5.86%	5.42%
65	7.02	6.47	5.96	65	6.75	6.32	5.88
70	8.04	7.31	6.65	70	7.46	7.01	6.59
75	9.53	8.73	7.68	75	8.33	7.93	7.45
80	11.90	10.87	9.35	80	9.30	8.96	8.51
85	15.17	14.27	11.70	85	10.08	9.95	9.45
90	20.10	19.34	14.51	90	10.66	10.49	9.86

Exhibit 7, Volume 2, CFA Curriculum CFA
Source: www.immediateannuities.com (retrieved December 2014).

Annuity pricing also depends on yields available on bonds, as insurance companies tend to invest conservatively. When current yields on bonds are lower than historical bond yields, annuity payouts will be low compared with historical averages. If life expectancy is rising at the same time, then payouts will be even lower.

2. **Immediate variable annuity:** The annuitant trades a single lump sum of money today in exchange for a promised income benefit for as long as the annuitant is alive. The income benefit varies over time, depending on the investment performance of the portfolio's underlying assets. During up markets, the payment will go up. During down markets, the payment will go down. The annuitant can purchase an income floor that provides protection during down markets. Without the floor, it is possible that payments could stop if the underlying assets fall to zero.

3. **Deferred fixed annuity:** The annuitant pays premiums on an ongoing basis prior to retirement and receives an annuity payout at some future date. At any time prior to retirement, the investor can cash out the accumulated funds, which may be subject to a surrender charge. At retirement, the annuitant can either cash out or annuitize the accumulated funds with a periodic fixed payment, with most investors choosing to annuitize.

4. **Deferred variable annuity:** The annuitant pays a premium on an ongoing basis prior to retirement and receives an annuity payout at some future date. The annuitant can choose from a menu of investment options, similar to the purchase of mutual funds. However, the annuity is purchased through a salesperson who is licensed to sell insurance products. Compared with mutual funds, deferred variable annuities can be more expensive and have limited investment options.

The surrender charge is usually a declining percentage over eight or so years, so more mature annuities may not be subject to the surrender charge.

Deferred variable annuities can include a death benefit to a beneficiary. In exchange for a fee, the insurance company will pay the entire amount used to purchase the annuity when the annuitant dies and the value of the contract is less than the initial investment. The annuitant can surrender his or her contract prior to retirement in exchange for a surrender charge. At retirement, the annuitant can simply start taking a variable income based on investment performance, add a contract rider, or annuitize the contract by converting it to an immediate payout annuity. Few investors actually annuitize a deferred variable annuity.

Without a rider, there is no guaranteed income stream for life, as the underlying investments could decrease in value until they are worthless. Then, the annuity payments would stop, possibly while the annuitant is still alive. A guaranteed minimum withdrawal benefit-for-life rider can be added to construct a guaranteed income stream for life. In up markets, the initial investment may not be depleted, and any remaining value will be paid to the beneficiary. If the investment value is depleted because of poor investment performance, the insurance company will continue to pay the minimum benefit until the annuitant's death.

5. **Advanced life deferred annuity (aLda):** An ALDA is a hybrid of deferred fixed annuity and immediate fixed annuity and is known as pure longevity insurance. In exchange for an immediate lump-sum payment, ALDA payments begin later in life well after retirement, typically when the annuitant turns 80 or 85. The premiums will be much lower than for an immediate payment annuity. There are three reasons for the lower premium: (1) the insurance company can earn a return on the initial lump sum before making the first payment, (2) life expectancy of a person who is 80 years old is much lower than a person aged 65 at a normal retirement age, and (3) the annuitant may die before payments are made.

LOS 14i: Discuss the relative advantages and disadvantages of fixed and variable annuities. Vol 2, pp 426–431

When selecting between fixed and variable annuities, there are a number of important considerations:

- **Volatility of the benefit amount:** Investors who have a high risk tolerance might be better suited to a variable annuity, while those who need assurance of benefit payouts are better suited for a fixed annuity.
- **Flexibility:** Immediate fixed annuities are irrevocable and cannot be undone. Variable annuities are tied to the investment performance of a subaccount, which can allow for withdrawals by the annuitant.
- **Future market expectations:** If the investor believes that the markets are going to perform better in the future, a variable annuity is a better choice than a fixed annuity. A fixed annuity locks the investor into a portfolio of bond-like assets subject to interest rate risk. An investor considering a fixed annuity who expects that interest rates will increase may defer purchasing the annuity until after rates increase. However, there is a risk that life expectancy will be longer in the future, resulting in lower payouts.
- **Fees:** Variable annuities tend to have higher fees than fixed annuities. Immediate fixed annuities are easier to compare with each other, an important feature when comparing annuity payouts among insurance companies.

- **Inflation concerns:** Fixed annuities are nominal payouts and do not change with inflation. However, a rider can be added to a fixed annuity to increase benefits in line with inflation. Some variable annuities automatically allow for payments to increase or decrease with inflation.

There are five payout methods:

1. **Life annuity:** Payments are made until the death of the annuitant.
2. **Period-certain annuity:** Payments are made for a specific number of periods, regardless of the life span of the annuitant.
3. **Life annuity with period certain:** Payments are made for the entire life of the annuitant or a minimum number of years (most common is 10 years) even if the annuitant dies. If the annuitant dies within the minimum number of years, payments continue to the beneficiary for the remainder of the period certain.
4. **Life annuity with refund:** This annuity guarantees that the annuitant or beneficiary receives payments equal to the total amount paid into the contract, which equals the initial investment less fees.
5. **Joint life annuity:** Payments continue for two or more annuitants, such as a husband-wife couple, as long as either one of them is alive. Payments stop when the surviving annuitant dies.

An individual can self-insure longevity risk by either making periodic withdrawals from one's own investment portfolio or annuitizing through a life insurance company. In an annuity, each payment is a combination of interest, principal (premium), and mortality credits. Mortality credits are benefits that surviving members of the annuity pool receive from those who have passed away. Self-insurers do not receive mortality credits, only the interest and principal. However, they face longevity risk.

Annuitants pay a higher price for insurance in exchange for the mitigation and possible elimination of longevity risk. In other words, in exchange for lower shortfall risk (lower risk of running out of money during one's lifetime) the investor has a lower wealth because of annuity premiums. This tradeoff, similar to an efficient frontier for a risky portfolio, is shown in Figure 6-1.

Figure 6-1   Retirement Income Efficient Frontier

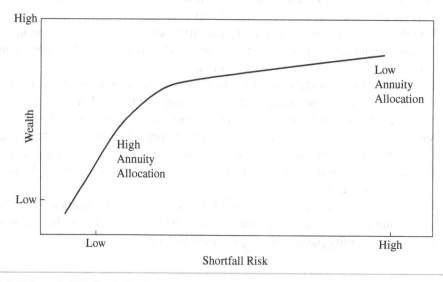

Exhibit 9, Volume 2, CFA Curriculum CFA 2019

The international shift away from defined-benefit (DB) pension plans has caused a shift toward annuities. At the individual level, there are five factors that would likely **increase demand** for any annuity:

1. Longer-than-average life expectancy
2. Greater preference for lifetime income
3. Less concern for leaving money to heirs
4. More conservative investing preferences
5. Lower guaranteed income from other sources (such as pensions)

LESSON 7: IMPLEMENTATION OF RISK MANAGEMENT FOR INDIVIDUALS

LOS 14j: Analyze and critique an insurance program. Vol 2, pp 431–440

LOS 14l: Recommend and justify appropriate strategies for asset allocation and risk reduction when given an investor profile of key inputs. Vol 2, pp 440–443

The decision to retain risk or buy insurance is determined by a household's risk tolerance. At the same level of wealth, a more risk-tolerant household will prefer to retain more risk, either through higher insurance deductibles or by simply not buying insurance. A risk-averse household would have lower deductibles and purchase more insurance. For all households, insurance products that have a higher load (expenses) will encourage a household to retain more risk. Finally, as the variability of income increases, the need for life insurance decreases because the present value of future earnings (human capital) will be lower with a higher discount rate.

Table 7-1 shows the appropriateness of the four risk management techniques depending on the severity of loss and the frequency of loss.

Table 7-1: Risk Management Techniques

Loss Characteristics	High Frequency	Low Frequency
High severity	Risk avoidance	Risk transfer
Low severity	Risk reduction	Risk retention

Exhibit 10, Volume 2, CFA Curriculum CFA 2019

An investment advisor will often be asked how much life insurance is enough. There are two techniques that you will be responsible for on the exam:

1. **Human life value method:** This technique estimates the present value of earnings that must be replaced.
2. **Needs analysis method:** This technique estimates the financial needs of the dependents.

Examples 7-1 and 7-2 demonstrate each method, respectively.

Example 7-1: Human Life Value Method

Life Insurance Needs for Jacques and Marion Examples, Volume 2, CFA Curriculum

As mentioned previously, the *human life value* method is consistent with the concept of human capital and involves replacing the estimated net contributions to family finances that Jacques would generate if he did not die during his projected earning life. Calculating these contributions involves the following steps:

- Start with the actual pre-tax compensation that Jacques would receive from employment: €100,000.
- Adjust for income taxation, and here we assume a 30% rate: €100,000 – €30,000 = €70,000 post-tax compensation.
- Adjust for family expenses attributable to Jacques that will not exist after his death, such as his transportation, travel, clothing, food, entertainment, and insurance premiums. Here, we assume those expenses to be €20,000. So €70,000 – €20,000 = €50,000 income after expenses.
- Add the value of any non-taxable employee benefits that the family will no longer receive, such as employer contributions to retirement plans, which we assume to be €15,000: €50,000 + €15,000 = €65,000.
- Estimate the amount of pre-tax income needed to replace that income on an after-tax basis. Note that the rate of taxation of annual income generated from life insurance proceeds may be different from the rate of taxation of Jacques's employment income, and marginal rates may be lower for lower incomes. Here, we assume a 20% tax rate: €65,000/(1 – t) = €65,000/(1 – 0.20) = €81,250.
- We then apply an annual growth rate, assumed here to be 3%, to consider the effects of inflation and career advancement over the full 20 years until retirement.
- Finally, we discount all the future cash flows back to the present at an appropriate rate, assumed here to be 5%.

Assuming the lost income replacement would be needed by Jacques's family immediately, the human life value calculation can be solved as the present value of an annuity due with growing payments (a so-called "growing annuity due"). Using calculator keystrokes for an annuity due with level payments, the growth of payments can be incorporated by adjusting the discount rate to account for the growth rate of earnings. The adjusted rate i can be calculated as follows, as long as the discount rate is larger than the growth rate: [(1 + Discount rate)/(1 + Growth rate)] – 1, or (1.05/1.03) – 1 = 1.94%. Thus,

- Set the calculator for beginning-of-period payments.
- $n = 20$ (the number of years until retirement)
- Payment = €81,250
- $i = 1.94\%$

Solving for the present value of an annuity due, the human life value method recommends €1,362,203 of life insurance for Jacques. Because Jacques already has €250,000 of life insurance, he should purchase an additional €1,112,203, according to this method.

This amount would likely be rounded to €1.1 million.

Example 7-2: Needs Analysis Method

Life Insurance Needs for Jacques and Marion Examples, Volume 2, CFA Curriculum 2019

The needs analysis method is concerned with meeting the financial needs of the family rather than replacing human capital. Needs analysis typically includes the following steps:

- Estimate the amount of cash that will be needed upon the death of the insured person. This amount will include final expenses (funeral and burial) as well as any taxes that may be payable. It is also common to pay off all debt (including mortgages) and to fully fund future education costs. An emergency fund should be created.
- Estimate the capital needed to fund family living expenses. This calculation requires discounting estimated living expenses (i.e., calculating the present value of future cash flow needs) during multiple time frames, typically as follows:
  - Estimate the surviving spouse's living expense needs, assumed here to continue for 52 years, until Marion is 90 years old. Note that when the mortgage and other debts are paid off, living expenses are lower.
  - Estimate the children's living expense needs, assumed here to continue until they are 22 years old. This amount does not include the education fund.
  - Include an additional amount for extra expenses during a transition period after Jacques's death, perhaps covering two years. In general, this period recognizes that there may be some contractual obligations, such as a car lease, that may not terminate upon a person's death.
  - Consider Marion's future income (earnings). Note, however, that Marion may prefer not to go back to work full-time as soon as planned because of the extra responsibilities of being a single parent. She may even choose to resign from her part-time job.
- Calculate total needs as the sum of cash needs and capital needs.
- Calculate total capital available, which may include cash/savings, retirement benefits, life insurance, rental property, and other assets.
- Calculate the life insurance need as the difference between the total financial needs and the total capital available.

Table 7-2 is a representation of a needs analysis for Jacques.

Table 7-2: Financial Needs: Life Insurance Worksheet

Cash Needs	Euro (€)
Final expenses	10,000
Taxes payable	5,000
Mortgage retirement	190,000
Other debt	10,000
Education fund	200,000
Emergency fund	30,000
Total cash needs	445,000
Capital Needs [present value of annuity due: growth rate = 3%, discount rate = 5%, adjusted rate (as above) = 1.94%]	
Marion's living expenses (60,000/year for 52 years)	1,991,941
Children's living expenses:	
Henri (10,000/year for 14 years)	123,934
Émilie (10,000/year for 16 years)	139,071
Transition period needs (10,000/year for 2 years)	19,810
Less Marion's income:	
Until Émilie is 16 (20,000/year for 10 years)	−183,713
Age 48–60 (60,000/year for 12 years)	−398,565[a]
Total capital needs	1,692,478
Total Financial Needs	**2,137,478**
Capital Available	
Cash and savings	30,000
Vested retirement accounts—present value	200,000
Life insurance	250,000
Rental property	165,000
Total capital available	645,000
Life insurance need	**1,492,478**
(Total financial needs less total capital available)	

[a] Calculated in two steps: (1) Compute the amount needed in 10 years, when Marion will begin earning €60,000 per year. Assuming 12 years of earnings from age 48 to age 60, a 3% annual growth in earnings, and a 5% discount rate (1.94% adjusted discount rate), a present value of an annuity due calculation shows that €649,220 will be needed in 10 years. (2) Discount the €649,220 back to the present—10 years at the unadjusted discount rate of 5%—for a total of €398,565. The discount rate is not adjusted during this period because there are no payments to which a growth rate would be applied. We simply discount a future value to the present.

The amount of additional life insurance under the needs analysis method would likely be rounded to €1.5 million, considerably higher than the €1.11 million calculated using the human life value method. The insurance amount selected depends on which method seems more relevant to the family situation, an average of the two amounts, or an amount that reaches a premium rate discount.

These are lengthy calculations, for sure. Please do not be tempted to skip them. If asked on the morning session of the exam, this could be worth 8 to 10 points, perhaps more points and a greater time commitment than questions associated with the required rate of return for an individual investor.

LOS 14k: Discuss how asset allocation policy may be influenced by the risk characteristics of human capital. Vol 2, pp 443–446

Human capital (that is, the present value of future expected earnings) is part of an investor's net wealth on the economic (holistic) balance sheet. High variability of expected earnings—such as with an executive in the oil and gas industry subject to volatile energy prices—will have increased risk associated with the value of the human capital asset. Risk associated with the value of human capital can be diversified by investing less in the employer's stock, and adding less risky and uncorrelated assets in the financial portfolio.

For a tenured professor, human capital is more bond-like and can benefit from the addition of risky financial assets such as equities.

Study Session 7: Portfolio Management for Institutional Investors

READING 15: MANAGING INSTITUTIONAL INVESTOR PORTFOLIOS

Time to complete: 2 to 3 hours

Reading Summary: This reading is one of the most important readings to master at Level III. Based on past morning session Level III exams, it is most likely that you will be asked to prepare at least one institutional IPS. Institutional investors are the large corporations, whether non-profit or for-profit, that have significant amounts of money to invest. Although some individual investors (e.g., Bill Gates) may have larger assets than many institutions, the issues of governance and investment policy are different for institutions than for individuals.

There are five broad classes of institutional investors: pension funds; foundations; endowments; insurance companies; and banks.

LESSON 1: INSTITUTIONAL IPS: DEFINED BENEFIT (DB) PENSION PLANS

PENSION PLANS

Pension plans are monies invested to provide retirement income to plan participants, also known as beneficiaries. The organization in charge of the fund—usually the employer of the plan participants—is known as the plan sponsor.

Pension plans come in different varieties, with different sets of considerations for the participants and the sponsors.

LOS 15a: Contrast a defined-benefit plan to a defined-contribution plan and discuss the advantages and disadvantages of each from the perspectives of the employee and the employer. Vol 2, pp 462–464

Defined-Benefit Plans

A defined-benefit (DB) plan is one in which the sponsor makes a promise of a specific payment to the plan participants. The benefit is defined by a formula commonly based on years of service with the employer and the employee's age. The employer's contribution will vary based on a range of factors, such as investment returns and average age of the employees.

- The future benefits promised under the plan create a pension liability that is only satisfied when the beneficiary dies. The plan sponsor has the investment risk; if returns are less than expected, then the plan sponsor will have to contribute more money to the fund.
- The benefit is defined based on what the employee will receive after retirement.
- The only risk the beneficiary has is that the plan is terminated, something many employers have done in order to reduce their liabilities.

Defined-Contribution Plans

Under a defined-contribution (DC) plan, the plan sponsor agrees to make a specific contribution to the employee's personal pension fund, but the ultimate benefit received in retirement will vary. The plan beneficiary bears the investment risk, and the sponsor's obligation is met once the contribution is made. Taxes are deferred, and the beneficiary will receive either a lump sum or a stream of payments upon retirement.

- The contribution is defined while the employee is working. It is how much the plan sponsor will contribute toward the employee's retirement. The employee owns the contribution and can generally take the plan assets to a new plan (subject to vesting schedules and tax laws). In other words, the plan is portable as the employee moves from employer to employer over the individual's career.
- The contribution may be a percentage of the worker's pay, a flat dollar amount, a match of the employee's own contribution, or a share of the firm's profits.

The plan sponsor has no liability in a defined-contribution plan. In some cases, the sponsor choses the investments (sponsor-directed plan); in others, the participant does (participant-directed).

LOS 15b: Discuss investment objectives and constraints for defined-benefit plans. **Vol 2, pp 464–477**

LOS 15d: Prepare an investment policy statement for a defined-benefit plan. **Vol 2, pp 464–477**

LOS 15e: Evaluate the risk management considerations in investing pension plan assets. **Vol 2, pp 464–477**

LOS 15f: Prepare an investment policy statement for a participant directed defined-contribution plan. **Vol 2, pp 464–477**

DEFINED-BENEFIT PLANS: INVESTMENT OBJECTIVES AND CONSTRAINTS

Defined-benefit pension plans have complex investment policies—certainly more complex than for defined-contribution plans—and usually more complex than for other types of institutional investors. Defined-benefit plans are becoming less popular in the United States because of the potential size of the pension liabilities and the complexity of managing them.

Defined-Benefit Pension Liabilities

Defined benefit pensions have several moving parts that must be considered before working on an investment policy statement. The assets in the fund have to pay for the benefits—the liabilities—that will be received in future years. These factors drive the investment objectives and constraints more than any other factors.

The liabilities are generally split between retired and active lives. The more people who are retired, the greater the cash flow demands on the fund (higher need for liquidity), but the shorter the duration.

Simply put, the plan assets are used to fund the plan liabilities.

Accumulated Benefit Obligation

The accumulated benefit obligation (ABO) is the present value of the plan benefits, calculated as if the plan were shut down today. It includes benefits accrued so far and excludes the effects of future wage increases.

Projected Benefit Obligation

The projected benefit obligation (PBO) looks at the present value of plan benefits assuming that the plan shut down today. Unlike accumulated benefit obligation, it includes the effects of wage increases that would affect the amount received in retirement.

Total Future Liability

Total future liability is the present value of accumulated and projected benefits, including the effects of future wage increases. Although this is the most comprehensive approach to finding pension liabilities, the calculation carries the most assumptions and thus has the most uncertainty.

Objectives

Investment objectives are the risk and return targets set for the fund. For a defined-benefit pension, risk management is paramount in order to ensure that the fund has enough assets to meet the liabilities.

Risk

The key risk management concern of a pension fund is how to match the assets with the liabilities. The risk objectives for a pension fund are affected by several factors, including:

LOS 15c: Evaluate pension fund risk tolerance when risk is considered from the perspective of the 1) plan surplus, 2) sponsor financial status and profitability, 3) sponsor and pension fund common risk exposures, 4) plan features, and 5) workforce characteristics. Vol 2, pg 466

- *Plan funding status*—if the fund has a surplus or a small liability, it can take more risk than a fund with a large liability.
- *Sponsor's financial status*—the lower the sponsor's debt-to-equity ratio on its balance sheet, the more risk the pension fund can take. Also, the higher the profitability on the sponsor's income statement, the greater tolerance of the pension plan.
- *Common risks between the pension fund and the plan sponsor*—the greater the correlation between the sponsor's operating profits and the pension fund's returns, the less investment risk the pension fund can handle.
- *Plan features*—if the plan offers such features and early retirement or lump-sum distributions, then the plan durations have a lower duration and can bear less risk.
- *Workforce*—the older the workforce and the greater the proportion of retirees, the shorter the duration of the plan assets and the less risk the pension fund can tolerate.

> These risk features have been heavily tested in the past with high weight. It is well worth the investment to know these well.

DEFINED-BENEFIT PLANS: STAKEHOLDERS AND RISK

Defined-benefit pension plans are separate entities from the sponsoring organizations, but they maintain a tight relationship. The financial health of one affects the financial health of the other. The sponsor needs to generate enough cash flow to meet the pension funding obligations. The pension funding obligations, in turn, are affected by the return generated by the plan's investments. This creates some tensions that should be considered in drafting the investment policy statement and managing the pension plan.

Plan Surplus

A key challenge for a defined-benefit pension plan's trustees is matching the pension liabilities with the plan assets. In a perfect world, the pension manager would ensure that the plan assets will be sufficient to meet the minimum plan requirements without additional contributions from the plan sponsor. In the real world, the plan manager wants to increase the probability of this happening.

If the fund is running a surplus, then the challenge is easier. The goal is to maintain the funded status by concentrating on the volatility of the surplus rather than the plan assets themselves.

Sponsor's Financial Status and Profitability

The absolute risk of the sponsor's business should also be considered. A sponsor in a risky industry may have a difficult time making large plan contributions, at least in some years. In this situation, the defined-benefit plan would have to have less risk in order to avoid the need for increased contributions.

Sponsor and Pension Fund's Common Risks

Evaluating the common risks starts by looking at the correlation between the pension plan's returns and the performance of the sponsor company. In general, a low correlation means that the pension fund has a higher risk tolerance.

Plan Features

Defined-benefit pensions would be simpler to manage if liabilities were based entirely on payments made to retirees over the course of their retirement at a predetermined age. Many plans have additional features, such as the opportunity to take a lump sum of cash instead of a regular stream of payments or to retire early and receive smaller benefits. All else being equal, these features will reduce the duration of the fund's liabilities. That, in turn, reduces the fund's risk tolerance.

Workforce Characteristics

When a worker is hired, he or she begins participating in a DB pension plan. Money is contributed each pay period into the pension fund, where it is invested. When the worker retires, the money in the plan is used to fund a payment each month during retirement until he or she dies.

The more years the employee works, the more money is contributed, the greater the investment returns, and the smaller the number of years in retirement. Hence, the demographic makeup of the pension fund's participants has a huge effect on the investment policy.

Active Lives

A plan that has a young workforce, with many years to retire, has less risk than one where the workers are closer to retirement age. There is more time for money to be invested, and the time until the plan will make large retirement payouts is further away. In this situation, a pension plan has a longer duration and a greater risk tolerance, all else being equal.

Retired Lives

The more plan participants who are retired, the more the pension plan must generate cash to cover the payments. This shortens a pension plan's duration and decreases the risk tolerance, all else being equal.

The proportion of active to retired lives is a critical ratio for a DB pension plan. The higher the ratio, the greater the tolerance to take risk, largely stemming from a longer time horizon and lower need for liquidity. From an asset allocation perspective, a rule of thumb is that equities are the best match for active lives and fixed income is the best match for retired lives.

Return

The return objective for a pension is simple: to generate enough total return to fund liabilities for the long term. For a plan that is fully funded, where assets equal liabilities, the discount rate determined by the plan's actuary will be the minimum return objective. Sometimes, it could be higher if the plan wishes to grow the surplus, provided that it is prudent to do so.

Constraints

The funding status of pensions, as well as the characteristics of the beneficiaries and the sponsors, determines the constraints. And there are many.

Liquidity

The liquidity constraint for a pension fund is based on how much cash the fund needs to pay out each month. The first source of cash will be money taken in that period in the form of contributions; if that amount is not adequate, then the investments will need to generate income or be liquidated. On the other hand, if contributions are greater than the current need for liquidity, the excess can be invested in order to generate future return.

Another factor that affects liquidity is the ability of plan participants to take early retirement or to take a lump sum out of the fund at retirement. These events both increase the need for cash on hand.

Time Horizon

For most pension plans, the time horizon is long term. It may also be described as a single stage to perpetuity. Two factors come into play: whether the plan is expected to continue or if it has a planned termination date, and the age of the workforce and the proportion of active lives, which will lengthen the time horizon.

Tax Considerations

In almost all cases, the investment income and capital gains of a defined-benefit pension plan are exempt from taxation, so there are no tax considerations.

Legal and Regulatory Factors

Retirement plans are governed by a series of regulations to ensure that the money is invested for the benefit of the plan participants and to maintain compliance with tax laws. The laws that apply vary greatly; many nations have several sets of regulations that apply in different provinces, for different types of employers, or for different play structures.

In the United States, for example, the primary regulation for corporate-sponsored defined-benefit pensions is the **Employee Retirement Income Security Act (ERISA)** of 1974. Government employees and union plans are covered by different laws. A defined-benefit pension plan's investment policy must reflect the applicable regulations for the plan in question. On the exam, if the plan is outside the United States, then you could say that it must meet ERISA-like rules.

Unique Circumstances

Obviously, the unique circumstances for each pension plan will be just that—unique. But there are a few that occur often enough that they deserve mention:

- The ability of the fund fiduciaries to perform adequate due diligence (research and investigation on the investment opportunity and the managers involved). For small funds, the lack of resources may mean that the plan assets cannot be placed in such complex investments as hedge funds or private equity.
- Socially responsible investment criteria, such as avoiding investing in the shares of companies that distill alcohol, cigarettes, guns, and munitions.

DEFINED-CONTRIBUTION PLANS: INVESTMENT POLICY STATEMENTS

The IPS for sponsor-directed DC plans is similar to that for defined-benefit plans. The IPS for *participant-directed* DC plans, however, must accommodate each individual's objectives and constraints. Toward that end, participant-directed DC plans in the U.S. must offer at least three investment options with diversification against each other and allow free movement among the options. Limitations on allocation to company stock (where that is an option) are common.

Purpose of the Investment Policy Statement

The defined-contribution investment policy statement needs to:

- Separate the responsibilities of the plan overseers, the plan participants, the investment managers, and the trustee/record-keeper contracted by the plan overseers.
- Describe the investments available to the plan participants.
- Discuss how investment manager performance is evaluated.
- Discuss the process for investment manager selection, termination, and replacement.
- Establish communication procedures.

Plan Overseer Roles and Responsibilities

The plan overseer may be members of the human resources department of the sponsoring employer, but it may be a committee with representatives of the HR departments, managers, and employees. No matter what group is put in charge, its roles and responsibilities should be defined to include:

- Selecting investments so that plan participants can meet their own investment objectives and build diversified portfolios.
- Monitoring investment performance relative to fees and adjusting the investment manager mix as appropriate.
- Providing education and ongoing communication to plan participants.
- Selecting and monitoring the work of the plan trustee and record-keeper, replacing if necessary.
- Setting the interest rate for any loans allowed by the plan in accordance with the plan provisions.

Plan Participant Roles and Responsibilities

Plan participants often have no specialized investment experience, and they need to be aware that choosing their own contribution levels and investments carry much responsibility.

- Learning about the plan and its features.
- Making an asset allocation decision that is appropriate for the employee's age, income, time until retirement, risk tolerance, accumulation objectives, retirement income objectives, and other factors that may be important.
- Determining how much money to contribute each year in order to fund the investment objective.

LOS 15g: Discuss hybrid pension plans (e.g., cash balance plans) and employee stock ownership plans. Vol 2, pp 483–484

You will not be asked to prepare IPS for these types of plans. We include these plans just in case they are mentioned as background information and for context on the exam.

HYBRID PENSION PLANS AND EMPLOYEE STOCK OWNERSHIP PLANS

A hybrid pension plan is a cross between a defined-benefit and a defined-contribution pension plan. These are becoming more common due to different state and municipal employees pension plan reforms. Examples of hybrid plans include cash balance plans, pension equity plans, target benefit plans, and floor plans.

The versions that deserve special mention are cash balance plans and employee stock ownership plans.

Cash Balance Plans

With a cash balance plan, the employer is responsible for investing the plan assets. Unlike a defined-benefit plan, though, the employee receives regular statements showing their account balances, their annual contribution credits, and their earnings credits.

In most cases, a cash balance plan is created by converting a traditional defined-benefit plan in order to give workers some of the benefits of a defined-contribution plan. This may benefit younger workers more than older ones, so it can be controversial.

Employee Stock Ownership Plans

An employee stock ownership plan, also known as an Employee Share Ownership Plan or ESOP, is a way to allow employees to save money for retirement or another goal through investment in the company's shares. Some of these plans allow employees to buy shares with pretax dollars, while others allow them to buy shares through the company with payroll after taxes. Buyers may receive a discount off the market price, making participation more attractive.

Some ESOPs are set up as defined-contribution pension plans. The contributions are made before taxes and are based on a percentage of the employee's pay. The final value is then available to the employee for use in retirement.

An ESOP gives workers a stake in the place where they work, but it also exposes them to risk to their financial and human capital. If the company fails, the worker will lose both employment and retirement savings.

LESSON 2: INSTITUTIONAL IPS: FOUNDATIONS

LOS 15h: Distinguish among various types of foundations, with respect to their description, purpose, and source of funds. Vol 2, pp 484–485

FOUNDATIONS

A foundation is a charitable institution that invests money and collects gifts to distribute in the form of grants to different non-profit organizations. They have many different goals and time horizons. There are four primary types of foundations:

- An **independent foundation** may be established by an individual or a family. The donors or trustees make the decisions, and they give grants to social, educational, charitable, or religious organizations. At least 5% of the 12-month annual asset value must be spent for philanthropic purposes, in addition to the investment expenses. The foundation's grant-making overhead counts toward the philanthropic spending, but investment operations do not.
- **Company-sponsored foundations** receive money from a corporation but are legally independent. The corporation donates money out of its profits, and its executives usually control the board of trustees. At least 5% of the 12-month annual asset value must be spent for philanthropic purposes, in addition to the investment expenses.
- **Operating foundations** use the money from investments to conduct research or provide a direct philanthropic service rather than give grants to other organizations. They have an independent board of directors and must use 85% of interest and dividend income to support their programs each year.
- **Community foundations** have many donors who come from the public at large. The money is invested and given as grants to social, educational, charitable, or religious organizations. They have no annual spending requirement.

> On the exam, you will be asked to prepare an IPS for either an independent or company-sponsored foundation. Both of these foundations have the same objectives and constraints

An **endowment** is a long-term fund that is related to a foundation, although its structure is different. An endowment is owned by a non-profit institution such as a university, museum, or hospital and used to provide support for its mission. These are often funded by many people, and the money is usually considered to be in place for perpetuity. True endowments have no minimum or maximum spending requirement as long as the asset value does not fall below the amount that was originally donated.

Example 2-1

A successful technology entrepreneur decides to set up a private foundation that will support arts and music programs in public schools. Her plan is to make grants for 20 years, then liquidate the foundation and give the money to universities that provide scholarships for arts and music education. Which of the following would you *most* expect to find in the foundation's investment policy statement?

A. "The Foundation will be managed for maximum capital appreciation in order to have significant principal at the time of liquidation."

B. "Funds should be invested in low-risk assets in order to meet the grant requirements."

C. "Assets should be managed in order to maintain enough liquidity to meet the mandated 5% spending requirement."

Solution:

C. The priority is to meet the spending requirement. Beyond that, the fund may seek capital appreciation, but that is not the primary priority. Furthermore, a portfolio may hold more than low-risk assets and still meet the spending requirement.

Many organizations also hold funds in an account that is considered to be an endowment but that has a different legal status. These quasi-endowments, also known as Funds Functioning as Endowments (FFEs), have no spending limits and may be liquidated.

LOS 15i: Compare the investment objectives and constraints of foundations, endowments, insurance companies, and banks. Vol 2, pp 489–527

LOS 15j: Discuss the factors that determine investment policy for pension funds, foundation endowments, life and non-life insurance companies, and banks. Vol 2, pp 489–527

LOS 15k: Prepare an investment policy statement for a foundation, an endowment, an insurance company, and a bank. Vol 2, pp 489–527

LOS 15l: Contrast investment companies, commodity pools, and hedge funds to other types of institutional investors. Vol 2, pp 489–527

LOS 15m: Compare the asset/liability management needs of pension funds, foundations, endowments, insurance companies, and banks. Vol 2, pp 489–527

LOS 15n: Compare the investment objectives and constraints of institutional investors given relevant data, such as descriptions of their financial circumstances and attitudes toward risk. Vol 2, pp 489–527

OTHER INSTITUTIONAL INVESTORS: INVESTMENT OBJECTIVES

Foundations

Foundations are non-profit institutions that have been established by a wealthy donor to make grants to charities. The focus of our discussion is on two types of foundations: private (or family) and company-sponsored foundations. The IPS treatment is the same for both types.

Return Objectives

There are three components in the return objective for a foundation:

1. a minimum spending rate of 5% of the investment portfolio plus
2. annual inflation rate plus
3. investment management expenses (fees).

Note that the foundation's minimum spending requirement of 5% is needed so that the foundation does not pay tax on its investment returns. You could also mention this is as a tax constraint, which is discussed later. Most foundations want to maintain or increase their support for charitable organizations over time.

As an example, consider a foundation that faces annual consumer price inflation (CPI) of 2.5% and annual investment management fees of 0.50%. The minimum return requirement would be:

- Minimum spending rate of 5% plus
- CPI of 2.5% plus
- Annual investment management expenses of 0.50%
- The additive total is 8.0%

You could also use the more theoretically correct technique of computing the geometric return: $[(1 + 0.05)(1 + 0.025)(1 + 0.005)] - 1 = 8.16\%$. In past morning sessions of the Level III exam, the guideline answers have included both techniques. Whichever technique you choose, make sure that you show your work when asked.

Risk Objectives

Compared with an DB pension plan, foundations generally have high risk tolerance because they have no defined legal liability.

However, in considering risk of a foundation by itself or compared with that of another foundation, watch for these factors:

- **Time horizon**: this can be infinite for a foundation that is established into perpetuity or shorter for foundation that is established for a finite period of time. The risk tolerance of a foundation with an infinite time horizon is higher than a foundation with a fixed time horizon. Moreover, the risk tolerance of the foundation with the fixed time horizon decreases over time. You must watch for the time horizon on the exam for a foundation: the donor has the option of setting it up forever or for a shorter fixed period.
- **Smoothing rule**: because investment returns may show much volatility, many foundations base spending off of an average asset valuation rather than the asset valuation at any point in time. For example, spending may be based off of the average asset value for the last five years rather than the year-end value. Without a smoothing rule, spending is more volatile, which reduces the ability of the foundation to take investment risk.
- **Past performance**: weak past performance, where the real inflation-adjusted return has been below the spending rate, plus investment management fees, will reduce the real value of the investment portfolio, which reduces the risk tolerance. In fact, the most appropriate step might be for the foundation set up in perpetuity to decrease its spending rate to maintain **intergenerational neutrality**, so that there is a balance between spending for current charities and future donations.
- **Ongoing donations**: if the foundations will receive donations, then this will increase the risk tolerance (and decrease liquidity needs). Alternatively, a reduction or termination of donations will cause the risk tolerance to decrease (and increase liquidity needs).

Liquidity

At a minimum, a foundation needs to have enough cash on hand to meet its spending requirement; so many foundations stick to the minimum spending requirement set by taxing authorities, which is 5% plus annual investment management expenses. *Do not add the inflation rate to the liquidity requirement.*

Many foundations want to have additional cash on hand in order to meet unexpected spending needs, just like an individual investor might like to hold emergency cash.

Time Horizon

Some foundations are managed under the assumption that the funds will be in place for perpetuity, with the time horizon set accordingly. Some foundations are designed to be spent down over a period of time, so the time horizon becomes shorter as the end date nears. The longer the time horizon, the more investment risk the foundation can bear. On the exam, you will be told whether the foundation is established in perpetuity or for a fixed time horizon.

The foundation can have a single stage time horizon if there are no expected changes to the future spending rate or can have a multi-stage time horizon if there are anticipated spending changes.

Tax Concerns

The foundation does not pay any tax on investment returns provided that it spends at least 5% of the portfolio value each year plus investment management expenses. (Should a foundation spend less than 5% in a given year, it may make it up by spending more than 5% in the next year. Likewise, if a foundation spends more than 5%, it is allowed to spend less in future years as long as the 5% long-term average holds.)

Watch for:

- **Unrelated business income:** If a foundation has income that is not related to its charitable purposes, then it will be classified as unrelated business income and that income is subject to corporate income taxes. For example, if a foundation whose charitable mandate is to improve the lives of people in developing countries also owns a company that makes vaccines, then that company's income is not subject to corporate taxes. The foundation may also own real estate, and rent from real estate that is financed with debt is taxable.

Legal and Regulatory Factors

Foundations are subject to the Uniform Management of Institutional Funds Act (UMIFA). UMIFA's standard of care is that of an ordinary business person, not a specialist investment professional.

Unique Circumstances

Many foundations are funded with a gift of stock from one particular company, and the donor may place a restriction on selling the stock in order to create a diversified portfolio. (This gives the foundation voting control, which may be important if the donor also controls the foundation.)

LESSON 3: INSTITUTIONAL IPS: ENDOWMENTS

Endowments

Endowments are non-profit institutions that have been established to provide operational support for a university or college, private school, hospital, museum, or religious organization. In past Level III exams, the institution supported by an endowment has typically been a university.

Return Objectives

The return objective for an endowment is similar to that of a foundation, with the exception of a specific inflation rate, which might be related to higher education costs or health care costs, both of which tend to increase higher than the consumer price index:

There are three components in the return objective for a foundation:

1. a spending rate determined by the endowment (there is no minimum spending rate) plus
2. specific inflation rate of the institution that the endowment supports plus
3. investment management expenses (fees).

A secondary return objective relates to the amount of budget support that the endowment provides to the institution that it supports. For example, a private university may not have any external funding sources, and the spending rate covers 100% of the university's spending budget. Be sure to watch for this secondary return objective as it will also affect the endowment's risk tolerance.

Risk Objectives

The following factors affect the risk of an endowment:

- **Operational needs of the institution:** The endowment contributes a significant portion of the organization's annual spending, then the endowment has a lower tolerance for risk.
- **Donor base:** If an economic contraction causes both a decline in investment returns and a decline in new donations, then the endowment has less ability to take investment risk.
- **Fixed costs:** If the organization has high fixed costs and relies on the endowment to help cover it, the endowment will have less risk tolerance than otherwise.
- **Time horizon:** By definition, the time horizon is infinite, so this is a factor that will tend to increase the risk tolerance.
- **Past performance:** This is the same as for foundations, explained above.
- **Public visibility:** The higher the public profile of an endowment, the lower the risk tolerance as staff and trustees might not like increased scrutiny when investment returns are low.

Smoothing rule: This is the same as for foundations, explained above. However, we add some detail to various examples of smoothing rules:

- **Simple spending rule:** The amount to be spent is the spending rate multiplied by the market value of the endowment at the beginning of the fiscal year.
- **Rolling three-year average spending rule:** The spending rate is multiplied by the average market value of the endowment at the end of the last three fiscal years.
- **Geometric smoothing rule:** Here, the spending rule is the weighted average of the prior year's inflation-adjusted spending and the product of the spending rate times the market value of the endowment at the beginning of the prior fiscal year. The advantage is that it allows the organization to incorporate spending into the budget before the current year's market value is known.

Liquidity

This is similar to a foundation, where the annual liquidity needs is the annual spending rate plus investment management fees. However, these can be offset by any donations.

Time Horizon

Because endowments are in place for perpetuity, the investment time horizon is infinitely long. However, the portfolio needs to accommodate near-term spending needs, so it must have enough liquid assets on hand to do that. Don't expect to be reminded on the exam that the endowment is established into perpetuity. You will be expected to know this. If there is no expected change in the spending rate, then the endowment faces a single stage time horizon.

Tax Concerns

Endowments are owned by non-profit organizations, so they are exempt from taxation on investment income. Like a foundation, they are also subject to tax on unrelated business income.

Legal and Regulatory Factors

Like a foundation, endowments are subject to UMIFA.

- The fund's governing board must exercise ordinary business care and prudence when dealing with investments.
- Endowment spending must respect any donor restrictions.
- The fund should not spend the original gift value, if it is structured as a true endowment rather than a fund functioning as an endowment.

Unique Circumstances

Endowments come in a huge array of sizes, and they are overseen by staff and board members with a wide range of investment experience. Very small endowments should consider the limits of size and expertise when setting investment policy.

Because of the perpetual status, many endowments invest in alternative asset classes, but this requires significant expertise to manage well.

Many endowments follow socially responsible investment (SRI) mandates.

LESSON 4: INSTITUTIONAL IPS: LIFE INSURANCE AND NON-LIFE INSURANCE COMPANIES (PROPERTY AND CASUALTY)

Insurance Companies

There are two types of insurance companies: life insurance companies and non-life insurance companies, which are also known as property and causality companies. In past morning Level III exams, whenever insurance companies have been tested, the focus has been on life insurance companies. This is also our focus, too. However, we will make key comparisons and contrasts where necessary.

A life insurance company sells three different types of products mainly to individuals: life insurance, which can either be whole life or term life, annuities, and guaranteed investment certificates (GICs). For the most part, the dollar amount of each liability is known and the timing and amounts of liability payments are estimated by an actuary. Generally, the liabilities of a life insurance company are long-term and sensitive to interest rates. The liabilities are known as policyholder reserves. The life insurance business tends to be stable over the business cycle, and claims are paid almost immediately when they come due.

A property and casualty insurance company offers protection mainly to companies against various risks, such as marine shipping or to the aviation industry. Of course, there are individual risks to be covered as well, such as house and car insurance. The key difference is that these liabilities have uncertain timing and uncertain cash flows and tend to have shorter durations. These liabilities are not interest rate sensitive but are inflation sensitive. Property and casualty business is sensitive to the business cycle, which leads to what is called the underwriting cycle. Underwriting new business is higher during economic expansions. During recessions, underwriting losses are common, which puts more pressure on the investment portfolio to make up for operating shortfalls. Finally, it may take years to report, process, and pay a claim, known as the "long tail," which is unique to property and casualty companies.

Return Objectives

Life insurance companies earn the net interest spread, which is the difference between the interest earned on the investment portfolio and the return to policyholder reserves. The investment objective is to maximize the amount of the spread.

For property and casualty insurance companies, as the liabilities are unknown, they do not try to maximize a spread. Instead, the return objective will be to maximize the return on capital. If the liabilities can be defined, then the return will be expressed as to maximize the return on surplus (assets minus liabilities).

In addition, property and casualty insurance companies want to earn enough of a return in the investment portfolio so that they can price policies competitively. If a company has large losses, it will have to charge more, and that will drive customers to competitors.

Risk

Insurance companies exist to pay claims. The policyholders pay the insurance company, which then invests the money until a claim is made and it has to pay out. Because insurance is an important part of risk management in almost all sectors of the economy, insurance companies are expected to take a conservative approach to risk when structuring their own portfolios. For example, life insurance companies in the United States are expected to maintain an asset-valuation reserve (a liability on the company's balance sheet) in order to protect against declines in investment losses.

Key investment risks for life insurance companies include:

- **Valuation concerns:** Interest rates affect the valuation of the assets and the liabilities. When interest rates change, there can be a mismatch in duration of the assets and liabilities that erodes the surplus. Specifically, *if the duration of assets is greater than the duration of liabilities*, the surplus will erode when interest rates increase. Alternatively, if interest rates decrease, the surplus will increase, *if the duration of assets is greater than the duration of liabilities*

- **Reinvestment risk:** Insurance companies heavily invest in fixed-income securities. If they have to reinvest principal and interest at a rate below where it was issued, then returns will decline. Reinvestment risk increases in a declining interest rate environment.
- **Credit risk:** Investments in fixed-income securities may decline in value if the borrower has financial distress. Widening credit spreads result in higher credit risk.
- **Cash flow volatility:** Insurance companies want to earn interest on cash held in reserve, and that means that problems collecting or reinvesting cash flow will have a negative effect on the company. If the investment portfolio contains callable bonds or mortgage-backed securities, then an increase in interest rates will decrease estimated cash flows (fewer bonds called and slower prepayments, respectively) and increase cash flow volatility risk.

> Whenever life insurance companies have been tested on the exam, at least two of the four risks have been tested with a high weight.

Liquidity

For the most part, a life insurance's company cash inflows exceed cash outflows, so liquidity is not a significant issue. As a result, insurance companies tend to have portfolios with long time horizons. Nevertheless, there are situations where liquidity is an important consideration.

- **Disintermediation** is the term for investors moving from low-return assets owned through financial institutions to high-return assets purchased in the general market. If rates of return increase in the market, many people will surrender their life insurance policies and invest money on their own to self-insure against risk. This is especially true in the life insurance market, where many policies are sold as much as investment products as insurance products. *Life insurance companies face higher disintermediation when interest rates are rising*.
- **Asset marketability risk** is a concern because many insurance company assets are held in illiquid assets that may not be sold quickly. If companies experience a high level of claims or of disintermediation, then illiquid assets may have to be sold at a discount.
- **Long-tail risk** at casualty insurance companies, because some risks may play out over decades. For example, environmental or occupational health hazards may not come to light for many years, but the insurance company is expected to have resources on hand to cover such insured risks. Life insurance companies do not face long-tail risk.

Time Horizon

The time horizons of different types of policies (say, auto insurance or group life) may be matched with assets that have a similar time horizon in order to better manage asset-liability risk. This is known as portfolio segmentation. Generally speaking, the time horizon for a life insurance company is longer than that for property and casualty companies because the liabilities of a life insurance company have longer durations.

Tax Concerns

Both life insurance and property and casualty insurance companies pay taxes. The amounts levied vary by jurisdiction.

Legal and Regulatory Factors

Both types of insurance companies are highly regulated in order to protect against a loss of principal that would leave customers unable to receive money for their claims. In most countries, insurance companies are expected to maintain minimum risk-based capital (RBC) levels to ensure that there is enough surplus to cover risks to both assets and liabilities.

Finally, in the United States, life insurance companies are required to maintain an asset valuation reserve of high-quality, liquid assets to protect the surplus from declining illiquid asset values. Property and casualty companies are not required to maintain an asset valuation reserve, so the surplus takes the full impact of declining illiquid asset values.

Unique Circumstances

Although some companies may have their own idiosyncrasies, there are no typical unique circumstances in this industry.

LESSON 5: INSTITUTIONAL IPS: BANKS

Banks

Return

If the bank has more funds than needed to meet loan demand, then it will want to invest those funds in order to generate a return that contributes to the bank's profits. Despite all of the constraints and all of the risk factors that affect banks, the object is to earn a spread in the investment portfolio in excess of the liabilities.

Risk

To manage the risks of assets (loans and securities) and liabilities (deposit accounts), banks pay considerable attention to interest rates. The two key measures are *net interest margin*, which is (interest income – interest expense)/average earning assets, and *interest spread*, or the average yield on earning assets – average cost of interest-bearing liabilities.

Three key measures of risk, to be considered in most bank investment policy statements, are:

- **Leverage-adjusted duration gap**, which measures a bank's overall interest exposure. The leverage-adjusted duration gap is defined as $D_A - kD_L$, where D_A is the duration of assets, D_L is the duration of liabilities, and $k = L/A$, the ratio of the market value of liabilities (L) to the market value of assets (A). *In a rising interest rate environment, a positive leverage-adjusted duration gap will cause the bank's net worth on its balance sheet to decrease.*
- **Value at risk (VAR)**, which is the minimum value of losses expected over a specified time period at a given level of probability.
- **Credit risk**, or the repayment risk included in the bank's loan portfolio. If the credit risk of the bank's loan portfolio is too high, then the credit risk of the investment portfolio can be lowered.

Liquidity

Regulatory limits on bank investments force liquidity. Beyond that, liquidity requirements are determined by the rate of net outflows of deposits and the demand for loans.

Time Horizon

The time horizon for a bank's investments is driven by the need to manage interest rate risk. Most banks keep the time horizon between three to seven years—an intermediate term—to manage the shorter maturity of deposits than of loans.

Tax Concerns

Bank portfolios are taxable.

Legal and Regulatory Factors

Banks are highly regulated, both nationally and internationally.

In the United States, banks have a pledging requirement, meaning that they must maintain government securities as collateral against uninsured deposits.

Under the Basel Accords, a global banking standard, banks have capital limits based on risk (also known as risk-based capital). The amount of capital that must be maintained is based on the credit risk of the bank's assets, whether those assets are included on the balance sheet or not.

Unique Circumstances

Although some banks may have their own idiosyncrasies, banks sometimes have moral obligations to support the communities that they operate in.

INVESTMENT COMPANIES, COMMODITY POOLS, AND HEDGE FUNDS

The financial services industry includes many other types of institutional investors beyond those discussed already.

These include funds that must file prospectuses with the Securities and Exchange Commission: open-end mutual funds, closed-end mutual funds, unit investment trusts, exchange-traded funds; and those that deal almost exclusively with investors who are allowed to invest in unregistered funds: hedge funds and commodity trading pools. Each of these funds has different risk and return objectives as well as different sets of investment constraints.